Countdown
to Christmas

Countdown to Christmas

Edited by Mary Cadogan

with photography by Marie-Louise Avery

Contents

For my husband, Mick

ACKNOWLEDGEMENTS

Many thanks to all the wonderful *Good Food* team, especially Orlando Murrin, Angela Nilsen, Vicky Musselman, Nicola Kelly and Lynne Stanford who gave me such great support during the planning, testing, writing and photographing of this book. I would also particularly like to thank Joanna Farrow who supplied the recipes on pages 16, 17, 28, 42, 54, 55, 66 and 68.

Recipes marked with this symbol are designed to be given as gifts

Introduction

I have been preparing family Christmas feasts for over twenty-five years, but the magic never wears off. I absolutely love being in the country at this time of year– still, clear, frosty mornings, gathering holly and mistletoe from the hedgerows, fire blazing in the hearth– but I know all too well that the hectic preparations can very often leave the cook feeling exhausted. In this book I will be sharing with you my hints and tips for creating the perfect Christmas, and will show how a little time spent planning ahead will help ensure a much more enjoyable Christmas for the cook.

If you have never hosted Christmas before, this book will guide you through all the dishes you are likely to need, from the easiest Christmas cake you will ever make, to the essential recipes for Christmas lunch itself. Advice is given on everything from how to prepare and cook your turkey to making perfect gravy and preparing delicious vegetables that are cooked to perfection. To help ensure that everything reaches the table on time, we have included a detailed timeplan which will take you right through from turning on the oven to sitting down to a delicious lunch. To make life even easier, we have added an essential shopping list – at such a busy time it is so easy to forget a crucial ingredient.

Whatever entertaining you are planning to do over the festive season, this book will provide all the answers. I challenged *Good Food*'s favourite celebrity chefs to come up with some extra special Christmas recipes and the mouth-watering dishes they created are all included here. What could be more perfect for a cosy dinner party than Ainsley Harriott's Roast Pork with Chilli Mango Stuffing, followed by either Chocolate Chestnut Log, or a glamorous Mango and Almond Trifle? And if you are having vegetarian friends round for a festive meal, Gary Rhodes' Vegetarian Christmas Feast is the perfect solution.

For the more experienced cook, the recipes in this book provide plenty of inspiration. Recipes from top chefs include a stunning dinner party menu that freezes beautifully: Tony Tobin devised a deceptively simple Chicken and Clementine Tagine and to follow Paul Rankin created a fabulous Chocolate Mousse Cake – a definite challenge, but worth every minute of your time.

To help you plan your time more easily we have started our countdown twelve weeks before Christmas and suggested what you may like to make each week. Of course everybody's schedule is different, what you see here is just a framework that you can easily adapt to your own needs. If you find, for example, that you haven't made the Christmas pudding eleven weeks in advance, don't worry, you can make it on Christmas Eve if that suits you better; it will still taste wonderful. Many of the recipes include information on preparing ahead and freezing, so you can work out your own timetable if you prefer. Making Christmas easier and more enjoyable is the purpose of the countdown, not to load you with guilt if you haven't managed to cook everything you had planned. Use it in the way you find most helpful and if you run out of time, cheat like mad.

Of course making your own of everything is a fantastic goal, but I hope this book will give you the confidence to plan your Christmas in a way that suits you best. If you prefer to buy your cranberry sauce and brandy butter, but would willingly spend hours decorating the cake, that's your choice and if it works for you, that's great. I am sure you will find, though, that making as many things as you can in advance means you are not left trying to do everything at the last minute. Make sure you get the rest of the family to lend a hand so that Christmas can be a pleasure for all, especially the cook.

Scattered throughout the book are gift ideas for food-loving friends. I particularly enjoy making edible gifts and spending time wrapping them beautifully, especially when I know they will be greatly appreciated and enjoyed by the recipient. Something that you have made yourself and spent precious time and effort on will always give special pleasure. Save or buy beautiful jars to show off Cranberry and Clementine Marmalade or to fill with Phil Vickery's Red Onion and Apricot Chutney, and pour Rosemary and Lemon Oil into elegant bottles with hand written labels. Home-made Chocolate truffles are a perfect gift if you are visiting friends for a meal and our Christmas pudding also makes a lovely present, particularly if you make a round one. Wrap in the usual way, then overwrap in cellophane and tie with a wide gold or silver ribbon. Don't forget to attach a label giving re-heating and storage instructions.

Finally, if you're on a special diet, or cooking for someone who is, there's no need to go without those seasonal classics: the mince pies and the Christmas Pudding. We have included some gluten-free recipes that are full of festive flavour.

I hope that, by using this book, the run-up to Christmas will be a more pleasurable experience for everyone and, most of all, I hope that it will help you enjoy the best Christmas ever.

Best wishes for a very happy Christmas.

Mary Cadee-

Countdown Calendar

If you're following our countdown, by the time November arrives you will already have made your Christmas cake, pudding and mince pies. There are still, however, a lot of jobs to be done, so to guide you through the final hectic weeks, use this calendar as a basis for your preparations.

NOVEMBER

1 Go through the cupboards to make way for all the Christmas food.

2 Do the same with the freezer.
Plan a couple of meals to use up the things you discover.

3 Make and freeze Lesley Waters' Freeze-ahead Spicy Cigars (page 22).

4

5 Check you have enough plates and glasses.

6

7 Make a shopping list of things to buy now such as food basics, matches, candles, paper napkins and kitchen foil.

8 Make and freeze the Chocolate Chestnut Log on page 26.

9

10 If you want a boozy Christmas cake, remember to keep feeding it weekly with brandy.

11

12 Decide what drinks you will need over the festive season and make a list of things to buy.

13

14 Order the turkey. Turn to page 92 to decide on the right size.

15 Make Phil Vickery's delicious Red Onion and Apricot Chutney (page 30).

16

17

18 Make and freeze the dough for the Stilton and Walnut Crunchies (page 28).

19

20

21

22

23 Make the first part of the Freeze-ahead Dinner Party – Tony Tobin's Chicken and Clementine Tagine (page 34).

24

25 Buy the Christmas Crackers while there is still some choice.

26

27 Make Paul Rankin's Chocolate Mousse Cake to round off the freeze-ahead menu (page 38).

28 Shop for wines, spirits and mixers. Arrange delivery if possible.

29

30

DECEMBER

1

2

3 Cook Glazed Ham with Caramelized Fruits (page 42) for supper with friends. Leftovers are perfect for a cold lunch.

4

5 Update your shopping lists. Plan what is still needed for everyday cooking, entertaining and Christmas food.

6 If you're entertaining vegetarians, make and freeze Gary Rhodes's Vegetarian Christmas Feast (page 46).

7

8 Order extras from the milkman such as cream, juice and mineral water. (Less to carry home.)

9

10 Make the marzipan stars for the cake and leave to dry (Starry Christmas Cake, page 52).
Invite friends round and serve-up your Freeze-ahead Dinner Party menu.

11

12 Decorate the Christmas cake.

13 Make and freeze the Cranberry Sauce (page 51).
Freeze the breadcrumbs for the bread sauce.

14

15 Make the Brandy Butter (page 50) to serve with the Light and Crumbly Christmas Pudding (page 12).

16

17

18 If you're having a drinks party, prepare the canapés (page 60).

19 Cook the Stilton and Walnut Crunchies (dough already made and frozen)
Make the Pistachio Chocolate Brittle (page 54) and the Super-rich Chocolate Truffles (page 55).

20

21 Make the Festive Almond Biscuits (page 68).
Wrap-up all the edible gifts ready to give as presents.

22 Defrost your Festive Mince Pies (page 20) ready for any visitors.

23 Shop early for all the last-minute fresh food.
Make Ainsley's Roast Pork with Chilli Mango Stuffing for a special dinner (page 70). Serve the Chocolate Chestnut Log (already made and frozen) for pudding.

24 Collect the turkey.
Stuff the red onions (page 86) .
Make the Sausagemeat and Thyme Koftas (page 88).
Prepare the Mango and Almond Trifle (page 74) as an alternative to Christmas pudding.
Make the Lemon and Lime Butter for the turkey (page 84).

25 Follow the timeplan (page 83) for your perfect Christmas lunch.

Moist  and Fruity
Christmas Cake

This cake keeps for up to three months – made now, it will be in perfect shape by Christmas. Fabulously moist and buttery, it's packed with all the wonderful Christmassy fruits and spices – not to mention the alcohol. (If you want a non-alcoholic cake, replace the brandy or sherry with the same amount of orange or apple juice.) The mixture is made in a saucepan, which saves on washing-up.

225 g/8 oz butter, chopped, plus extra
    for greasing
300 g/10 oz dark muscovado sugar
2 × 500 g bags luxury mixed dried fruit
finely grated rind and juice of 1 orange
finely grated rind and juice of 1 lemon
125 ml/4 fl oz brandy or sherry
100 g packet whole blanched almonds
4 large eggs, lightly beaten
100 g packet ground almonds
300 g/10 oz plain flour
½ teaspoon baking powder
1 teaspoon mixed spice
1 teaspoon ground cinnamon
½ teaspoon freshly grated nutmeg

Preparation: 1½ hours
Cooking: 3–3½ hours
Makes: a 20 cm/8 in round or 18 cm/7 in square cake

One Put the butter, sugar, dried fruit, citrus rinds and juices, and brandy or sherry in a large pan and bring slowly to the boil, stirring until the butter has melted, then reduce the heat and let it bubble gently for 10 minutes, stirring occasionally (picture 1). Meanwhile cut a double-thickness strip of greaseproof paper 5 cm/ 2 in deeper than your cake tin and long enough to wrap around the tin with a slight overlap. Make a 2.5 cm/1 in crease along the long folded edge, then snip the paper up to the crease at regular intervals. Cut 2 rounds or squares of paper to fit the base of the tin (draw around the tin with a pencil on to double-thickness paper, then cut along the pencil line). Grease the tin, then line the base with one piece of paper. Grease the paper then fit the long strip of paper around the sides with the snipped edge flat on the base of the tin. Grease the paper and fit the second piece of paper over the top. Preheat the oven to 150°C/Gas 2; fan oven: cook from cold at 130°C.

Two Remove the pan from the heat and leave to cool for about 30 minutes. Toast the whole almonds in a dry frying pan, tossing them until they are evenly browned (this helps to bring out the flavour). When cool enough to handle, chop them roughly. Stir the eggs, and the chopped and ground almonds, into the cooled fruit mixture and mix well. Set a sieve over the pan and sift the flour, baking powder and spices into the pan (picture 2). Stir in gently but thoroughly until there are no traces of flour left.

Three Spoon the mixture into the tin and spread it out evenly (picture 3).

Four Dip a large metal spoon into boiling water, then smooth over the cake mixture to level. Bake for 1 hour, then reduce the heat to 140°C/Gas 1/fan oven 120°C and bake for a further 2–2½ hours until the cake is dark golden and firm to touch. Cover the top with foil if it starts to darken too much.

Five To see if the cake is ready, insert a fine skewer into the centre – if it comes out clean the cake is cooked (picture 4). If it is not cooked, return to the oven for 15 minutes, then test again. Repeat until the cake is cooked. Allow the cake to cool in the tin for 15 minutes, then turn out, peel off the paper and cool on a wire rack. Wrap in double-thickness greaseproof paper, then overwrap in foil.

✱ FEEDING THE CAKE: For a more boozy cake, feed it with extra brandy after baking. Invert the cake and make holes all over the base with a fine skewer. Spoon 2 tablespoons of brandy over the holes until it soaks in. Rewrap cake and repeat weekly until ready to ice (see my Starry Cake on page 52).

✱ STORING THE CAKE: Store the cake, well wrapped in double-thickness greaseproof paper and overwrapped in foil, in a cool dry place – damp warm conditions could turn it mouldy. Any leftover cake can be frozen up to a year if un-iced, or up to 3 months if iced.

Light and Crumbly
Christmas Pudding

This Christmas pudding is just the way I like it – moist, crumbly, not at all dark or heavy – and made with butter instead of suet to give it a better flavour. And you can choose whichever fruits you like – not just the familiar ones. As a bonus, the pudding is steamed in the oven: you don't have to top up the water so often and the kitchen windows don't get fogged up. You can eat one pudding this year and save the other for next year; but if you want to make just one, then the ingredients are easily halved.

800 g/1 lb 12 oz mixed dried fruit
   of your choice, e.g. dates, figs,
   apricots, glacé cherries,
   currants, raisins, cranberries
   or pineapple
grated rind and juice of 1 lemon
grated rind and juice of 1 orange
125 ml/4 fl oz brandy or sherry
225 g/8 oz softened butter, plus
   extra for greasing
225 g/8 oz dark muscovado sugar
4 eggs, lightly beaten
50 g/2 oz blanched almonds,
   toasted and chopped
100 g/4 oz self-raising flour
1 teaspoon each of mixed spice,
   nutmeg, ginger and cinnamon
100 g/4 oz fresh white breadcrumbs

Preparation: 30 minutes, plus up to 4 days soaking

Cooking: 3–4 hours

Makes: two 1.2 litre/2 pint puddings, each enough for 8

14

One If any of the dried fruits you are using are too large, chop them into smaller pieces (picture 1).

Two Put the mixed fruit, citrus rinds and juices, and brandy or sherry in a large bowl, stir and cover with a tea towel; leave for 2–4 days, stirring occasionally (picture 2).

Three Preheat the oven to 160°C/Gas 3; fan oven: cook from cold at 140°C. Butter two 1.2 litre/ 2 pint pudding basins and line the bases with a circle of greaseproof paper. Beat together the butter and sugar until the mixture is pale and fluffy; this should take about 5 minutes in a food processor, or 10 minutes by hand. Transfer to a large bowl. Gradually beat in the eggs, beating well after each addition – don't worry if the mixture curdles as it won't affect the taste.

Tip in the fruit, soaking liquid and almonds, and stir well. Get the family to help and everyone make a wish. Sift flour and spices, add breadcrumbs, and fold in well.

Four Fill the pudding basins with the mixture to within 2.5 cm/1 in of the top. Cover each with double-thickness greaseproof paper, pleated in the centre; tie down with string. Do this by wrapping a doubled length of kitchen string around the top rim of the basin. Thread one end through the loop and tie with a double knot, pulling it tightly to lock in place. Overtie to secure in place (pictures 3, 4). Trim off the excess paper, then overwrap with foil, tucking it under the greaseproof. Put the basin in a large roasting tin and pour in about 5 cm/2 in of boiling water (picture 5).

Five Cover the tin with a double-thickness tent of foil, sealing the edges tightly (picture 6). Bake for 3–4 hours until the puddings have risen, are firm to the touch and darker. You may have to top up with water.

✱ PREPARING AHEAD: This pudding can be made up to a year before you eat it. After the initial steaming, remove the foil and paper and replace with fresh. Store in a cool dry place, labelling it with the date you made it. Every couple of months feed with a tablespoon or two of brandy or sherry (see the tip on page 11). Reheat as above.

✱ TOASTING NUTS: Cook almonds in a dry frying pan over a low heat for 5 minutes, swirling the pan now and then so they brown evenly.

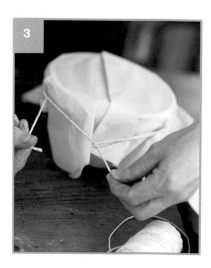

✱ TO REHEAT THE PUDDING: Replace the paper and foil. Lower one pudding into a large pan; pour in boiling water to come a third of the way up the basin. Cover tightly and steam for 2 hours. Or reheat in the microwave: remove the foil and microwave in a 750W oven on Medium for 6–8 minutes; leave to rest for 2 minutes.

✱ TO MAKE A ROUND PUDDING: Use half the recipe to fill a 900 g/2 lb mould and the full quantity for a 1.8 kg/4 lb mould. Liberally butter both halves of the mould. Put the mixture in one half of the mould and pile it up in the centre. Cover with the other half and lock into place. Steam as above.

✱ HIDING CHARMS: If you're hiding charms in the pudding, add them just before reheating. Sterilize them or wrap in foil first.

Cranberry and Clementine
Marmalade

This softly set marmalade will ensure you are thought about every breakfast time. It keeps unopened for up to 4 months, so you'll have plenty of time to plan when to make it; once opened, it should be used within a month.

600 g/1 lb 5 oz clementines

4 lemons

225 g/8 oz fresh or frozen cranberries

1.6 kg/3½ lb preserving or granulating sugar

150 ml/¼ pint whisky

Preparation: 25 minutes
Cooking: 1¼–1½ hours
Makes: about 2.2 kg/5 lb

One Halve the clementines and lemons and squeeze the juice (reserve the pips). Tie the pips and lemon halves in a piece of muslin. Thinly or thickly slice the clementine rind, removing any pith; put in a preserving pan. Add the squeezed juice, the muslin bag and 1.2 litres/2 pints water.

Two Bring to the boil, then simmer gently for 1 hour or until the peel is tender. Remove the muslin bag, squeezing out the juice.

Three Add the cranberries and cook for 2 minutes until they start to break up. Add the sugar, stirring until dissolved. Stir in the whisky.

Bring to the boil and boil rapidly for 20–35 minutes until setting point is reached. (Spoon a little of the liquid on to a saucer and chill for a few minutes. The mixture should wrinkle when pushed with your finger.) Leave the mixture to stand for 15 minutes. Ladle into sterilized jars. Seal well.

✱ HOW TO WRAP IN STYLE: Stand each glass jar inside a square cardboard box and stuff the spaces with scraps of tissue paper to protect the jars. Wrap the box in a large square of muslin, tied in place with wide gingham ribbon. Tie on a small spoon as a clue to the contents.

Rosemary and Lemon Oil

Flavoured oils are so versatile and make great gifts. They can be used in marinades and salad dressings, or splashed over bruschetta, roasted vegetables and fish. Choose small glass bottles with tight-fitting caps, as flavoured oil doesn't keep as long as unflavoured.

long sprigs of fresh rosemary

lemons

dry or brined pink
   peppercorns

olive oil

Wash and dry the rosemary sprigs and lemons. Push several rosemary sprigs down to the base of each bottle. Pare several strips of lemon rind and push them down into the bottle too. Dry the peppercorns on kitchen paper if using brined, then scatter a teaspoonful into each bottle. Pour in the olive oil, filling up to the rim, and replace the stopper.

Before giving as presents, allow 1–2 weeks for the flavours to blend.

✱ HOW TO WRAP IN STYLE:
A simple wrapping is all you need to disguise the bottle. Cut a length of baking parchment or Japanese hand-made paper the same width as your bottle is high, and long enough to wrap around it twice. Wrap it round the bottle, securing with a piece of sticky tape. Cut a length of wide dark green or brown organza ribbon (enough to go twice around the bottle). Tie in place with green garden string and tuck in a few sprigs of rosemary.

Preparation: 5 minutes

Cranberry and Orange
Mincemeat

This melt-in-the mouth mincemeat is fruitier and less sweet than traditional mincemeat – there's no suet in it, which lightens the texture too. It's perfect made now for Christmas, kept in a cool, dark place. Or, of course, you could use it now if you decide to make and freeze your own mince pies ahead of time – see the following recipe for Festive Mince Pies.

1 kg/2 lb 4 oz cooking apples

1 teaspoon mixed spice

1 teaspoon ground cinnamon

200 g/8 oz dark muscovado sugar

grated rind and juice of 3 oranges

grated rind and juice of 1 lemon

350 g/12 oz mixed dried fruit

100 g/4 oz dried apricots, chopped

350 g/12 oz cranberries, fresh or frozen

175 g/6 oz toasted flaked almonds

300 ml/½ pint brandy, rum or sherry

✱ TO KEEP LONGER: This mincemeat is not meant to be kept indefinitely – if you want to store it for more than 4 weeks pack it in small boxes in the freezer for up to 6 months.

✱ WHY COOKING APPLES? Cooking apples such as Bramleys cook to a smooth fluffy pulp, while eating apples tend to keep their shape. The apple pulp makes a smooth flavoursome base for the dried fruits, nuts and spices and means there is no need to add suet to keep the mincemeat moist.

One Peel, core and chop the apples, then put in a large pan with the spices, sugar, citrus rinds and juices. Bring to the boil, then cover and simmer for about 10 minutes until the apples start to soften. Add the dried fruit, apricots, cranberries, almonds and brandy, rum or sherry. Bring to the boil, stirring well, then reduce the heat and simmer for 10 minutes.

Two Remove from the heat, leave to cool, then pack the mincemeat into warm, sterilized jars, seal, label and keep for up to 4 weeks in a cool dry place.

Preparation: 30 minutes
Cooking: 20 minutes
Makes: about 1.8 kg/4 lb

Festive
Mince Pies

Here are some mince pies with a difference, using my Cranberry and Orange Mincemeat.

FOR THE PASTRY

200 g/8 oz plain flour

50 g/2 oz ground almonds

140 g/5 oz butter, chopped
  into small pieces

grated rind of 1 orange

50 g/2 oz caster sugar

1 egg yolk

FOR THE FILLING AND DECORATION

200 g/8 oz mincemeat

1 egg white, lightly whisked

caster sugar, for dusting

One Preheat the oven to 200°C/Gas 6/fan oven 190°C. Put the flour, almonds, butter, orange rind and sugar into a food processor and whizz into crumbs. Add the egg yolk and a teaspoon of cold water and pulse until it forms a dough. Wrap in plastic film and chill for 30 minutes.

Two Roll out the dough thinly and stamp out 18 × 7.5 cm/3 in rounds (picture 1). Use to line one and a half 12-hole bun tins.

Three Put a heaped teaspoon of mincemeat in each pastry case. Stamp out nine more, slightly smaller rounds to cover the pies. (You may need to scrunch up pastry trimmings, knead briefly and roll out again to get all the rounds you need.) Using small cutters, cut out stars, trees or other festive shapes from the centre of each round.

Four Cover half the pies with the shapes and the other half with the pastry rounds with the centres removed. Brush the pastry tops with egg white and dust lightly with caster sugar. They can be frozen at this stage, uncooked, in the bun tins, then removed and packed into freezer bags. (Freeze for up to 3 months.) Bake the pies from frozen for 18–20 minutes until the pastry is crisp and golden. Cool in the tins for 5 minutes, then remove and cool completely on a wire rack. (If you're not freezing the pies, then bake for 12–15 minutes.)

✱ MERINGUE PIES
Using half the quantity of pastry, roll and stamp out 12 rounds. Put a heaped teaspoon of mincemeat in each case. Whisk one egg white until stiff, then whisk in 50 g/2 oz golden caster sugar until the mixture forms stiff peaks. Spoon a little meringue on to each pie to seal in the filling and bake as before (picture 2). Do not freeze.

✱ MARZIPAN STAR PIES
Make half the pastry to line 12 bun-tin holes. Fill with mincemeat. Roll out 85 g/3 oz marzipan and stamp out 12 small stars or trees. Put on each pie and bake or freeze as before. Dust with icing sugar to serve.

✱ SPICE CRUMBLE PIES
Make the pastry without adding the egg and water. Put a quarter into another bowl and stir in 2 teaspoons of mixed spice and 50 g/2 oz flaked almonds. Add the egg yolk and 1 teaspoon of cold water to the remaining pastry mix, and stir to form a dough. Roll out and line 18 bun-tin holes. Fill with mincemeat, then sprinkle over the crumble. Bake or freeze as before.

Preparation: 25 minutes
Cooking: 12–15 minutes
Makes: 18

LESLEY WATERS'

Freeze-ahead
Spicy Cigars

Forget traditional sausage rolls – this elegant, lightly spiced version is fabulous at drinks parties or as an instant starter. The cigars freeze easily to keep for Christmas, though as they're so delicious you might like to make double the quantity and enjoy them before then! They're especially good served with a cooling mint raita dip.

Lesley Waters' lively personality makes her a great favourite on *Ready Steady Cook* and *Food and Drink*. Her varied career includes working as head teacher at Leith's School of Food and Wine in London and she is also the author of several cookery books. Lesley has a real talent for creating recipes that are just that bit different – often lighter, spicier and healthier. Her low-fat menus are regularly featured in *Good Food Magazine*.

Preparation: 30 minutes
Cooking: 20 minutes
Makes: 32

FOR THE CIGARS

250 g/9 oz Cumberland sausagemeat

25 g/1 oz ready-to-eat dried apricots,
   finely chopped

8 large filo pastry sheets,
   each 40 × 30 cm/16 × 12 in

1 egg, beaten

sesame seeds and paprika, for sprinkling

mint raita dip and watercress salad to serve

FOR THE SPICY PASTE

2 tablespoons grapeseed or sunflower oil

1 large onion, finely chopped

1 garlic clove, crushed

1 teaspoon ground cardamom

1 teaspoon ground coriander

1 teaspoon allspice

4 teaspoons paprika

1 teaspoon ground ginger

good pinch of cayenne pepper

1 teaspoon salt

freshly ground black pepper

One Preheat the oven to 190°C/Gas 5; fan oven: cook from cold at 170°C. Make the spicy paste: heat the oil in a frying pan with a lid. Add the chopped onion and cook covered over a low heat for 5–7 minutes until softened and golden. Add the remaining paste ingredients (picture 1) and season well with black pepper. Turn up the heat and fry for a further 30 seconds (picture 2). Transfer to a blender or small food processor with 2 tablespoons of cold water and whizz until smooth. Set aside. In a bowl, mix together the sausagemeat and apricots.

Two Lay 1 filo sheet on a work surface, top with another filo sheet and cut into 8 rectangles, 10 × 15 cm/4 × 6 in (picture 3). Spread each rectangle with half a teaspoon of spicy paste (picture 4).

Three Take a heaped teaspoon of the sausage and apricot mixture and shape it into a very thin sausage (picture 5). Lay the thin sausage across the bottom shorter edge of the rectangle, then carefully roll up in the pastry (picture 6). Transfer to a baking sheet lined with baking paper.

Four Repeat with the remaining ingredients to give 32 cigars.

Five Brush the cigars with beaten egg (picture 7).

Six Sprinkle with sesame seeds (picture 8). Bake for 15–18 minutes until the pastry is golden and crispy. Sprinkle with a little paprika 2 minutes before the end of cooking time. The cooked cigars are frozen at this stage: allow them to cool. Freeze on baking sheets until firm, then transfer to freezing bags or a freezerproof container. When you're ready, cook from frozen at 190°C/Gas 5/fan oven 170°C for 20 minutes.

Serve warm or cold with a mint raita dip, watercress salad and a drizzle of olive oil.

✱ MINT RAITA DIP
Grate half a cucumber, then mix with a 200 g tub of Greek yogurt and 3 tablespoons of chopped fresh mint.

Chocolate
Chestnut Log

200 g/8 oz dark chocolate, plus
   50 g/2 oz to decorate

200 g/8 oz unsweetened chestnut
   purée

5 tablespoons icing sugar

50 g/2 oz liquid glucose

425 ml/^{3}/$_4$ pint double cream

200 ml/7 fl oz double cream

200 ml/7 fl oz ready-made
   custard

25 g/1 oz icing sugar

1 teaspoon vanilla extract

This make-ahead frozen dessert is a rich but light
alternative to Christmas pudding. It's worth using
the best chocolate – the taste will really come
through. You can buy the liquid glucose from
chemists and larger supermarkets. It's sold in clear
jars and once opened keeps for several months.

Preparation: 20 minutes, plus 2 hours freezing

Serves: 8–10

One Line the base and sides of a 23 × 33 cm/9 × 13 in Swiss roll tin with a sheet of foil. Break up the chocolate and melt three-quarters in a bowl over a pan of hot water or in the microwave on Medium for about 2 minutes. Let the melted chocolate cool a little while you chop the remainder into chunks.

Two In a large bowl, beat the chestnut purée, sugar and glucose until well mixed (a hand-held mixer makes this job easier). Stir in the melted chocolate (picture 1). Whip the cream until stiff, then fold into the mixture, along with the chopped chocolate (picture 2). Spread the mixture evenly over the tin and smooth the top (picture 3). Freeze for 30 minutes until softly set.

Three Make the vanilla filling: whip the cream until stiff, then fold in the custard, sugar and vanilla. Spread evenly over the chocolate layer in the tin (picture 4) and freeze for 1–1½ hours, until the top layer is just firm.

Four Remove from the freezer (if the chocolate layer is too firm to roll up, leave for 10 minutes to soften slightly). Using the foil to help you, roll up from one short end (pictures 5, 6). Freeze the log on the tin, wrapped in foil, for 2 hours or until completely firm.

Five To decorate, break up the 50 g/2 oz chocolate and melt. Using a teaspoon or piping bag, quickly drizzle fine lines back and forth over the log. Freeze

uncovered until the chocolate has set. Wrap in greaseproof paper and overlap foil.

✱ TO SERVE: Remove this dessert from the freezer to the fridge about an hour before serving – by which time it should be soft enough to slice. If you serve iced desserts too cold, some of the flavour will be lost.

28

Stilton and Walnut
Crunchies

A great gift for those who like to linger over the cheese board, or enjoy a special savoury snack with drinks. You can choose just how far ahead to make these biscuits: the dough can be frozen for up to 2 months, then baked once thawed; or it can chill in the fridge for up to one week. Once baked, the biscuits will keep for up to 3 days in an airtight tin in a cool place.

Preparation: 15 minutes
Cooking: 15 minutes
Makes: about 30

225 g/8 oz plain flour

115 g/4 oz butter, cut into
   pieces, plus extra for
   greasing

140 g/5 oz Stilton

85 g/3 oz broken walnuts

2 egg yolks

beaten egg, to glaze

coarse salt, for sprinkling

One Put the flour and butter in a food processor and whizz briefly until the mixture resembles fine breadcrumbs. Crumble in 115 g/4 oz of the cheese and 50 g/2 oz of the walnuts. Whizz again briefly to mix. Add the egg yolks; whizz to a paste.

Two Preheat the oven to 180°C/Gas 4/fan oven 160°C. Grease 2 baking sheets. Roll out the pastry on a lightly floured surface to about 5 mm/$\frac{1}{4}$ in thick and stamp out 6 cm/$2\frac{1}{2}$ in rounds. Transfer to the baking sheet and prick lightly with a fork. Brush with beaten egg. Crumble the remaining cheese and scatter over the biscuits along with the coarse salt and reserved walnuts. Bake for 15–20 minutes until just golden. Cool on a wire rack.

✱ HOW TO WRAP IN STYLE: A long, narrow wooden box (about 25 cm × 9 cm × 11.5 cm) is just right for stacking biscuits in a neat row. Using pinking shears, cut two pieces of gold tissue paper to line the box, and tie with a gorgeous gold ribbon.

PHIL VICKERY'S

Red Onion and Apricot
Chutney

This fabulous fruity chutney is great with Christmas cold meats and cheeses. Make it now and it will be perfect for Christmas Day cold supper or Boxing Day. It makes a wonderful gift as well, packed into pretty jars, so you could double up the quantities if you like.

Phil Vickery, star of *Ready Steady Cook* and award-winning chef of the Castle Hotel in Taunton, is renowned for using seasonal produce. Whenever possible, he buys locally grown fruit and vegetables, meat from nearby farms and fish in its proper season. He loves bottling things away, particularly when there is a glut of summer fruits. When it comes to Christmas, he likes to use dried fruits and this is his favourite chutney recipe.

1 red chilli

3 medium onions

250 g/9 oz dried apricots, covered
with cold water and soaked overnight

100 ml/3½ fl oz olive oil

2 teaspoons cumin seeds

4 teaspoons white mustard seeds

2 teaspoons ground turmeric

2 garlic cloves, crushed

2 tablespoons caster sugar

2 teaspoons salt

200 ml/7 fl oz cider vinegar

100 ml/3½ fl oz white wine vinegar

freshly ground black pepper

Preparation: 15 minutes, plus
overnight soaking

Cooking: 40–50 minutes

Makes: 750 g/1 lb 10 oz

One Seed and finely chop the chilli using a small sharp knife. First remove the stalk, then cut the chilli in half down the length. Scrape out the seeds and discard. If you prefer a hotter chutney leave some in (picture 1). Peel and finely chop the onions (picture 2). Drain the apricots and cut into quarters.

Two Heat the oil in a stainless steel pan, then add the cumin, mustard seeds, turmeric, chilli and garlic (picture 3). Stir well, then cook gently for 2 minutes, stirring occasionally – do not allow the spices to burn (picture 4).

Three Add the onions, sugar and salt, and season well with black pepper (picture 5). Cook for a further 5 minutes until the onions have softened. Pour in the two vinegars and bring to the boil, then reduce the heat (picture 6). Add the chopped apricots and simmer gently for about 35–40 minutes until the chutney is thick and chunky. Season with salt and pepper to taste and allow to cool.

Four Spoon the chutney into jars (picture 7) and store in the fridge for about a week to allow the flavours to develop. The chutney will keep for up to 6 weeks stored in a cool place.

✱ DRIED APRICOTS: You can use ready-to-eat dried apricots, but soaking dried apricots overnight softens them further so they cook more quickly.

✱ PREPARING THE JARS: Use jars with a tight-fitting lid to give you a good seal. Kilner jars are perfect, or you can re-use pickle or jam jars. Check the lid is lined with plastic as the vinegar will react with metal. Preheat the oven to 150°C/Gas2/fan oven 130°C. Wash the jars thoroughly in hot soapy water, then carefully rinse and dry. Lay the jars in the oven for 15 minutes to sterilize, then remove and put on a board to fill them.

FREEZE-AHEAD DINNER PARTY TONY TOBIN'S

Chicken and Clementine Tagine
with Couscous

Make this sumptuous dinner party well in advance and freeze it until required – gourmet eating at a moment's notice. On the menu: Tony Tobin's Chicken and Clementine Tagine with Couscous, and Paul Rankin's Chocolate Mousse Cake. To make life even easier, you can divide the preparation over two weeks as suggested here. Make the Tagine one week, and then tackle Paul Rankin's delicious dessert the week after. That way you can spend more time on each dish.

Tony Tobin is well known for his wonderful way with flavour and his light modern approach to food. He doesn't believe in using excess cream in his cooking – his sauces are more likely to be based on flavoured oils, fresh herbs or vegetable purées than rich reduced gravies. This tagine is typical of his no-nonsense style, combining a few seasonal ingredients cooked simply but with care, to produce a delicious main course for a special meal. If you're cooking for four, then the ingredients can easily be halved.

2 onions

4 garlic cloves

2 teaspoons salt

juice of 1 lemon

1 bunch of fresh coriander

2 × 1.5 kg/3 lb 5 oz chickens, each cut into 8 pieces

2 teaspoons freshly ground black pepper

2 teaspoons ground ginger

½ teaspoon saffron filaments

125 ml/4 fl oz olive oil

1 cinnamon stick

12 clementines

350 g/12 oz pitted black olives

450 g/1 lb couscous

Preparation: 45 minutes, plus 30 minutes marinating

Cooking: 1 hour

Serves: 8

One Chop the onions very finely. Peel and crush the garlic.

Two Mix together the garlic, salt and lemon juice and chop half the coriander (picture 1). Add to the mixture, then rub into the chicken pieces in a large bowl (pictures 2, 3).

Three In a bowl, mix together the onions, black pepper, ginger, saffron and olive oil; pour over the chicken. Marinate for 30 minutes. Heat a large flameproof casserole or large pan. Remove the chicken pieces from the marinade, wiping off as much as possible (but don't throw the marinade away). Cook the chicken in batches until golden all over.

Four Return the chicken to the pan, then spoon over the marinade and add enough water to come two-thirds of the way up the chicken (picture 4). Add the cinnamon, bring to the boil, then reduce the heat; simmer for 30 minutes.

Five Wash but don't peel the clementines, then cut each into 8 wedges and add to the mixture (picture 5). Add the olives (picture 6) and simmer for 30 minutes. The dish is frozen at this stage: leave to cool and then transfer to a freezerproof container. (This can be kept frozen for up to 3 months.) To serve, defrost thoroughly, then put in a pan and bring to the boil. Simmer for 25 minutes to thoroughly reheat; continue with next stage.

Six Make the couscous according to the packet instructions (see page 37); keep warm. Remove the chicken from the dish and, if necessary, boil the cooking juices to reduce to a sauce consistency; season. Pour over the chicken.

Seven To serve, spoon the couscous on to a large plate and make a well in the centre. Spoon the chicken, clementines and juices into the middle. Chop the remaining coriander and sprinkle over.

✱ PREPARING AHEAD: If you prefer not to freeze the dish, but still want some time in hand, then the cooked tagine should be cooled quickly, covered and left to chill in the fridge for up to 2 days. Bring gently back to the boil, then cover and keep at simmering point for 20 minutes.

✱ FOR FLAVOUR: Use really good quality olives for this recipe. Buy them loose at the deli counter, so you can taste them first.

✱ PREPARING COUSCOUS: Use quick-cooking couscous, widely available in supermarkets and delis. Tip the couscous into a large bowl and cover with a slightly greater volume of boiling water or stock. The grains need to be covered by at least 5 cm/2 in of water. Leave for 5–10 minutes, then fluff up with a fork and season well. Drizzle with a little olive oil just before serving. If you want to prepare it a little ahead, cook as above, then spread over an ovenproof dish and dot with butter or drizzle with olive oil. Cover the dish with foil and put in a warm oven for 15–20 minutes, after which time it will be even more light and fluffy. Fork up the grains before serving.

FREEZE-AHEAD DINNER PARTY PAUL RANKIN'S

Chocolate Mousse Cake

This delectable cake looks absolutely stunning. While it isn't as complicated to make as it looks, it's still quite a challenge with all the techniques involved, so make sure you have the kitchen to yourself and take your time. (And, of course, you can choose your time – this cake freezes beautifully for up to four weeks.)

Paul Rankin is a regular face on TV and, when not showing the rest of us how it's done, he's working in his Belfast restaurant, Roscoff. In fact, this recipe is restaurant standard – and Paul shows you exactly how to make it.

FOR THE BASE

25 g/1 oz icing sugar, plus extra for dusting

50 g/2 oz caster sugar

50 g/2 oz egg whites

4 rounded tablespoons ground almonds, lightly toasted

FOR THE MOUSSE

450 g/1 lb quality plain cooking chocolate, chopped

3 eggs

200 ml/7 fl oz custard (bought or home-made), at room temperature

450 ml/16 fl oz whipping cream

4 tablespoons Cognac or brandy

3 tablespoons finely chopped candied ginger

TO DECORATE

175 g/6 oz plain chocolate

175 g/6 oz white chocolate

single cream, to serve

Preparation: 2 hours, plus 30 minutes freezing

Cooking: 1½ hours

Serves: 10–12

MAKE THE BASE

One Preheat the oven to 120°C/ gas $1/2$; fan oven: cook from cold at 100°C. Line a baking sheet with non-stick baking paper and lightly draw a 20–22 cm/8–8$1/2$ in circle on it as a guide. Have a piping bag with a 1 cm/$1/2$ in plain nozzle ready.

Two Make the base: sift the sugars together into a bowl. In another bowl, whisk the egg whites until stiff. (It is better to use a balloon whisk or hand-held electric whisk as very few mixers can handle such a small amount.) Whisk in a tablespoon of the sugars until firm and glossy. Fold the ground almonds into the rest of the sugar, then carefully fold into the whisked whites with a metal spoon.

Three Put the mixture in the piping bag and pipe the mixture in a continuous spiral to fill the circle – start in the centre and work your way out (picture 1). If it does not reach, use a palette knife to lightly spread it. (It will only be about 1.5 cm/$1/2$ in thick.) Dust the meringue with a little icing sugar, then bake for 1$1/2$ hours until crisp and light golden. Try not to let the meringue get too brown (you may need to change shelves and turn it around in the oven.) Remove from the oven and leave to cool.

✱ TO MAKE A PIPING BAG: Take a 30 cm/12 in square of greaseproof paper and cut in half diagonally to make two triangles. Hold the centre of the longest edge with your finger, then curve one point around to reach the point opposite your finger to form a cone shape. Curve the opposite point until all three points are together. Jiggle them until you have a sharp point where your finger was. Fold over the three points several times to secure, then snip off the end to the required size.

Four Line a 23 cm/9 in spring-form tin with plastic film. Cut two strips of firm plastic, 33 × 7.5 cm/ 13 × 3 in (the kind of firm but flexible clear plastic that you see in document sleeves is fine); use to line the tin sides. Shave a thin layer off the top of the meringue; reserve the shavings. Put the meringue base into the tin.

MAKE THE MOUSSE

One Melt the chocolate in a bowl set over a pan of simmering water (the base of the bowl mustn't touch the water), then set aside to cool for about 15 minutes. Using a hand-held electric whisk, whisk the eggs in a bowl over the simmering water for about 8 minutes until light and fluffy and they leave a trail when the beaters are lifted out. Remove from the heat and whisk until thickened and increased in volume. Slowly whisk in the custard, then fold in the cooled melted chocolate.

Two In a bowl, whip the cream into soft peaks, then fold into the chocolate mixture with the brandy so it has the consistency of softly whipped cream. Divide the mixture evenly between three bowls. Fold the meringue shavings into one mousse, then fold the candied ginger into the second.

Three Pour the meringue mousse on top of the base in the tin and freeze for 10 minutes. Pour over the ginger mousse and freeze for 10 minutes. Finally, pour over the remaining mousse. Cover loosely with plastic film and chill for up to 2 days. The cake is frozen at this stage: open freeze in the tin until firm, then cover with freezer foil or plastic film. When you're ready, proceed with the next stage.

MAKE THE DECORATION

One Use 2 piping bags for the decorations (see tip above on how to make your own). Cut 2 ribbons of greaseproof paper, about 40 × 6 cm/16 × 2½ in, and lay on a baking sheet. Line another baking sheet with greaseproof paper and lightly draw triangles on it, using the template. You'll need 1 triangle per portion, so make about 15 to allow for breakages.

Two Melt the chocolates in separate bowls over two pans of barely simmering water, then put a little of each into two piping bags. Starting with the plain chocolate bag, scribble finely over each paper ribbon, then scribble in the other direction with the white chocolate. If necessary, repeat with each to strengthen the lines. The lines should be fine, but close together to create a filigree (picture 2). Chill until firm.

template

5

Three Pipe a line of plain chocolate around each triangle, then scribble inside with the plain, then the white (picture 3). Chill until firm. When completely chilled, lift them off the paper and pack into a box. They will keep in the fridge for several days. (The ribbons are more fragile, so keep on the tray.)

ASSEMBLE THE CAKE

One Carefully lift off the sides of the tin and peel off the plastic film and strips. Slide the cake on to a flat plate or a cakeboard. Take one chocolate ribbon strip from the fridge and, if too firm, rub the paper lightly with the palm of your hand until it is malleable enough to mould around the side of the cake; press it around the cake (picture 4). Use as much of the second ribbon to cover the remainder of the side of the cake as necessary, trimming off the excess with scissors – leave the paper on the ribbons until the last minute. Chill.

Two To serve, mark each cake portion lightly with a knife. Carefully remove the paper ribbons. Stick a triangle into each portion at a 45 degree angle (picture 5). Dip a long sharp knife into a jug of hot water and dry quickly before slicing. Serve with single cream.

Glazed Ham with
Caramelized Fruits

A glazed ham makes a wonderful centrepiece for a larger party and is one of the traditional dishes we associate with Christmas. This gammon joint is simmered with a clove-studded tangerine and flavourings, then skinned and scored. It is then dowsed with whiskey, studded with stem ginger and brushed with a honey and ginger glaze, before being served with a shallot and tangerine sauce, and caramelized fruits. Serve it hot with simple accompaniments such as creamy mash, red cabbage or leeks. Any leftovers can be served cold with pickles and salads.

Preparation: 25 minutes, plus overnight soaking (optional)

Cooking: 2½–3¼ hours

Serves: 8–10, with leftovers

FOR THE HAM AND GLAZE

2.7–3.6 kg/6–8 lb smoked or unsmoked boned gammon

4 tangerines, clementines or satsumas

15 whole cloves

8 shallots, peeled, left whole or halved if large

3 celery sticks cut into large pieces

6 bay leaves

⅓ bottle (250 ml/9 fl oz) bourbon or Irish whiskey

300 ml/½ pint chicken or ham stock

3 pieces of stem ginger plus 2 tablespoons ginger syrup

50 g/2 oz clear honey plus a little extra

85 g/3 oz demerara sugar

4 fresh figs

bayleaves to garnish

FOR THE SAUCE

4 shallots, peeled and finely chopped

235 g/1 oz butter

2 teaspoons cornflour

100 ml/3½ fl oz tangerine, clementine or

   satsuma juice (about 3 fruits)

squeeze of lemon juice

One Put the gammon in a large pan so it fits snugly. Halve a tangerine, clementine or satsuma and stud with cloves. Add to the pan with the shallots, celery, bay leaves and enough water to cover (picture 1). Bring to the boil, cover and simmer gently for the calculated cooking time (see page 45). Skim off any scum during cooking with a slotted spoon.

Two Remove the gammon from the water and allow to cool slightly, then remove the string. Using a sharp knife, carefully ease away the skin to leave an even layer of fat (picture 2).

Three Using the tip of the knife, score the fat in diagonal lines, one way only, to give a decorative finish. Transfer the scored gammon to a roasting tin.

Four Pour the whiskey all over the gammon (picture 3), then pour the stock into the pan.

Five Preheat the oven to 220°C/Gas 7; fan oven: cook from cold at 200°C. Finely slice the stem ginger and tuck it into the scores of the fat. Mix together the honey, sugar and ginger syrup in a pan and heat gently until slightly thinned. Brush half over the gammon (picture 4). Bake for 15 minutes until beginning to colour.

Six Remove the gammon from the oven and baste with the juices in the roasting tin (picture 5). Glaze with the remaining honey and ginger mixture and bake for a further 15–20 minutes, basting once or twice more, until golden and beginning to char around the edges.

Seven Halve the remaining tangerines, clementines or satsumas and the figs and brush the cut sides with a little honey. Heat a little oil in a frying pan and fry the fruits for about 2–3 minutes on the cut sides until caramelized (picture 6). When the ham is ready, transfer to a warm plate and surround with the fruits and bay leaves; keep warm.

Eight Make the sauce: fry the shallots in the butter for 2 minutes until soft but not brown. Blend the cornflour with a little fruit juice, then stir in the rest. Add the cooking juices to the shallots with the tangerine juice, lemon juice and pepper. Bring to the boil and cook, stirring, for 2 minutes. Serve in a warm sauceboat with the ham.

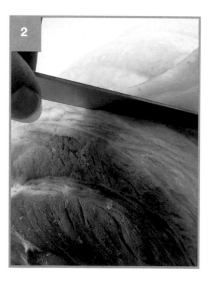

✱ CHOOSING A GAMMON JOINT: Gammon is the hind leg of the bacon pig after curing, but before cooking, and is available smoked or unsmoked – it's down to personal taste. Once cooked, it becomes ham. Allow about 225 g/8 oz raw weight per portion which usually provides plenty of leftovers. The joint should be tied with string when you buy it from the butcher but, if not, tie it yourself before cooking.

✱ DOES IT NEED SOAKING? Soaking removes excess salt. Mild cured gammon shouldn't need soaking, but if in doubt it's best to soak it in cold water for 24 hours before cooking, particularly smoked which tends to be more salty.

✱ CALCULATING THE COOKING TIME: Weigh the gammon joint, then allow 20 minutes cooking time per 450 g/1 lb, plus 20 minutes extra.

✱ WHY SHALLOTS? They have the bouquet of onions without the coarseness. Their sweet, delicate taste makes them useful for adding to sauces.

✱ LEFTOVERS: You can serve glazed ham hot or cold. It will keep in the fridge for up to 5 days for use in sandwiches and salads.

VEGETARIAN CHRISTMAS FEAST GARY RHODES'

Stilton Rarebit & Chestnut Bubble
with Roast Parsnips

This is a vegetarian's dream – a mash of flavoursome winter vegetables, topped with cranberry flavoured parsnips and served with a buttery sauce. This dish freezes well (for up to a month), if you don't want to eat it the same day you make it.

This is a typically inventive dish for Gary. A regular contributor to *Good Food Magazine,* his recipes are always stunning to look at and fabulous to eat. As Gary says, 'This has to be the ultimate vegetarian Christmas dish; it's got just about all the classic British flavours'.

Preparation: 2 hours
Cooking: 1 hour
Serves: 6

FOR THE RAREBIT

225 g/8 oz Stilton, chopped

100 g/4 oz Cheddar, grated

75 ml/3 fl oz milk

25 g/1 oz plain flour

25 g/1 oz fresh white breadcrumbs

½ tablespoon English mustard powder

1–2 shakes balsamic vinegar

1 medium egg, plus 1 medium egg yolk

FOR THE BUBBLE

450 g/1 lb Brussels sprouts, trimmed

   and thinly sliced

2 small onions, thinly sliced

50 g/2 oz butter

115–175 g/4 oz cooked chestnuts,

   chopped (or half 240 g can)

450 g/1 lb cooked potatoes, mashed

   without butter or milk

FOR THE PARSNIPS

25 g/1 oz butter

8–10 medium-sized parsnips

   (1.3–1.8 kg/3–4 lb), peeled,

   quartered lengthways and

   cores removed

3 tablespoons cranberry jelly

FOR THE SAUCE

150 ml/¼ pint reduced vegetable

   stock (either home-made

   or stock cubes)

squeeze of lemon juice

50–85 g/2–3 oz unsalted butter

1 teaspoon each chopped fresh

   parsley, sage and thyme,

   mixed together

✻ FOR FOUR PORTIONS: Use an 18–20 cm/
7–8 in diameter deep loose-bottomed round cake
tin with the base removed. You could also use a
20 cm/8 in baking ring, or even a large dish.

48

MAKE THE RAREBIT

One Put the Stilton and Cheddar in a pan with the milk. Heat gently until the cheeses have melted (don't let the mixture boil).

Two When the mixture is bubbling gently, add the flour, breadcrumbs and mustard. Cook for a few minutes, stirring over a low heat until the mixture comes away from the sides of the pan. Add the balsamic vinegar and leave to cool.

Three When cold, pour the mixture into a food processor, turn on the motor and slowly add the egg and egg yolk (picture 1). Once the eggs are mixed in, remove from the processor and wrap in plastic film, then put in a polythene bag and chill in the coldest part of the fridge while you prepare the rest of the dish.

MAKE THE BUBBLE

One Blanch the sprouts in boiling salted water for about 1 minute. Drain and refresh in iced water. Line a roasting tin with a double thickness of kitchen paper and put the sprouts in an even layer. Cover with 2 more sheets of kitchen paper and press firmly to dry the sprouts as much as possible.

Two Fry the onions in half the butter for 4–5 minutes until tender in a frying pan. Leave to cool.

Three Add the sprouts and chestnuts to the onions, then add the mashed potatoes a little at a time until the bubble is combined and firm. Season.

Four Liberally grease the cake tin or ring and an ovenproof frying pan with the remaining butter. Put the tin upside-down in the pan (the rim is now at the top so the cake can be removed easily) (picture 2). Spoon the bubble into the tin or ring; then press down. Shallow fry for 5–7 minutes so the base is golden and crisp. Set aside.

COOK THE PARSNIPS

One Preheat the oven to 230°C/Gas 8/fan oven 210°C. Heat the butter in a roasting tin over a moderate heat, then cook the parsnips for 10 minutes until golden. Season, then roast for 25–30 minutes.

Two The parsnips will now be crisp (almost overcooked) and deep golden brown, with a soft and creamy interior. While they are still hot lightly coat them in cranberry jelly.

Three The parsnips can now be packed on top of the bubble; put them end to end in concentric circles, starting at the edge of the ring and working inwards (picture 3). Pack them tightly together so the cake keeps its shape when the ring is removed. The cake can be frozen at this stage: open-freeze the whole dish in the tin before baking. Wrap in freezer film and freeze for up to a month. Defrost overnight in the fridge and continue with the next stage.

TO FINISH

One Preheat the oven to 200°C/Gas 6/fan oven 180°C. Put about two-thirds of the rarebit between two pieces of plastic film and roll into a disc the same diameter as the cake (this can be prepared in advance) (picture 4). Remove the plastic film and sit the rarebit on the cake. Bake in the ovenproof pan for 30 minutes until the cake is heated through and the top is golden brown (meanwhile, make the sauce). Remove the ring and cut into thick wedges. Serve with the herb butter sauce.

MAKE THE SAUCE

One Put the stock, lemon juice and 50 g/2 oz of the butter into a pan and bring to a simmer, whisking. Season. Whisk vigorously to give a light creamy consistency. If the sauce is too thin, then whisk in the remaining butter. Add the herbs just before serving.

✱ USING UP THE RAREBIT: This recipe doesn't use up all the rarebit, but it's difficult to make in a smaller amount because of the egg quantities. Wrap the remainder tightly in plastic film and it will keep in the fridge for up to a week. Use for a special cheese on toast, or put a little on the top of crisply baked slices of French bread and grill until bubbling. Or try a special post-Christmas hot open sandwich. Toast a thick slice of bread. Spread with mayonnaise, cover with slices of turkey and ham if you have it. Spread with cranberry sauce and cover with a thin layer of rarebit. Grill until bubbling and serve with a crisp salad and a glass of sherry. It's also really good on baked potatoes or as a topping for a pasta bake.

Brandy
Butter

Brandy Butter and Cranberry Sauce are quick to make and it is a good idea to get them out of the way now before things really start to hot up in the kitchen.

100 g/4 oz butter, softened

85 g/3 oz caster sugar

50 g/2 oz light muscovado sugar

4 tablespoons brandy

One Beat the butter until it is really soft and light, then beat in the sugars, a little at a time, beating well until the mixture is light and fluffy, about 5 minutes (picture 1).

Two Gradually beat in the brandy (picture 2). Spoon into a dish and rough up the top. Cover with plastic film and store in the fridge for up to 2 weeks.

Serves: 8

Cranberry Sauce

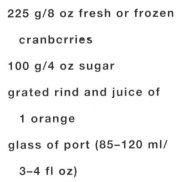

225 g/8 oz fresh or frozen

   cranberries

100 g/4 oz sugar

grated rind and juice of

   1 orange

glass of port (85–120 ml/

   3–4 fl oz)

One Put the cranberries in a pan with the sugar, the orange rind and juice (picture 1) and the port. Stir over a gentle heat until the sugar has dissolved, then simmer for 5–8 minutes until the cranberries are softened and the sauce has thickened (picture 2).

Two Allow the sauce to cool, then pour it into a rigid container. Keep in the fridge for up to a week or freeze for up to 2 months.

Preparation: 5 minutes
Cooking: 10–12 minutes
Serves: 10–12

52

Starry
Christmas Cake

700 g/1½ lb white marzipan
(450 g/1 lb if decorating the
top only)

25–28 cm/10–11 in cakeboard

apricot jam

2–3 egg whites

700 g/1½ lb icing sugar (450 g/
1 lb if decorating the top only),
plus extra for dusting

2 tablespoons liquid glucose
(buy from the chemist)

edible silver balls and wide silver
ribbon, to decorate

Your Moist and Fruity Christmas Cake (page 10)
should be well matured by now. This easy but
dazzling decoration is a fitting crown for it.

✱ PREPARING AHEAD: The stars can
be made up to 4 weeks before you
need them. Allow them to dry
completely and store in a food box,
interleaved with greaseproof paper.

One Roll out 225 g/8 oz marzipan on a board dusted with icing sugar. Cut out 20–25 stars with small and medium cutters (picture 1); put on a tray lined with baking parchment. Leave for 2 days.

Two Roll out a circle of marzipan to fit the top of the cake – a 20 cm/8 in round cake tin is the best guide (picture 2). To decorate the sides of the cake, cut a strip of baking parchment the same depth and length. Roll out the rest of the marzipan on the paper and trim to fit.

Three Put the cake on the cake board. Brush the top (and sides, if decorating) of the cake with jam (picture 3). Lay the marzipan circle on top (picture 4) (wrap the strip around the side, if using; peel off the paper).

Four Beat the egg whites lightly (2 for the top only, 3 for the top and sides), then gradually sift in the icing sugar, beating all the time until smooth and glossy. Beat in the glucose, then add enough icing sugar to form stiff peaks.

Five Spoon the icing on top of the cake, then swirl it over using a flat-bladed knife (picture 5). Spread it flat on the sides to make tying the ribbon easy.

Six Smear a little icing on the tips of the marzipan stars and stick on the silver balls. Stick the marzipan stars on to the cake (picture 6). Stick a few more silver balls on to the stars if necessary and sprinkle a few over the top of the cake. Leave to set, then tie the ribbon.

54

Pistachio  Chocolate Brittle

You can vary the nuts, but always use unsalted ones. These biscuits should be kept cool, or chilled, until you're ready to wrap them – they're best eaten within 2–3 weeks.

85 g/3 oz shelled unsalted pistachio nuts

175 g/6 oz milk chocolate

175g /6 oz white chocolate

350 g/12 oz plain chocolate

rice paper

One Cover the pistachios with boiling water and leave for 2 minutes. Drain and rub between sheets of kitchen paper to remove as much skin as possible. Pick off any remaining skin.

Two Roughly chop the milk and white chocolate. Break up 100 g/4 oz of the plain chocolate and melt in a bowl set over a pan of gently simmering water (or microwave on High for about 2 minutes). Remove from the heat.

Three Line the base and part way up the sides of a 20 cm/8 in square baking tin with rice paper. Spread the melted chocolate over the base and scatter with the chopped chocolate and pistachios. Melt the remaining plain chocolate and pour over. Leave to set.

Four Before wrapping, break into jagged pieces using the tip of a sturdy knife.

✱ PRESENTATION: The surface may develop a white bloom, like any chocolate bar – but don't worry. It doesn't affect the taste, and you can disguise it by dusting very lightly with cocoa powder.

✱ HOW TO WRAP IN STYLE: Take a 28 cm/11 in dinner plate with a plain coloured border and write a message using Pebeo Gold Cerne Relief, squeezed straight from the tube. Leave to dry. Arrange the brittle on a plate, overwrap with clear Cellophane and secure in a bunch in the centre with an elastic band.

Preparation: 20 minutes
Makes: about 800 g/1lb 12 oz

Super-rich
Chocolate
Truffles

An ideal gift for chocoholics – they're quick and easy to make and cheaper than shop-bought varieties. As they use fresh cream, they'll keep for only up to a week in the fridge.

150 ml/¼ pint extra thick double cream

300 g/10 oz good quality plain chocolate with at least 55 per cent cocoa solids, broken into pieces

3 tablespoons brandy, rum, or orange-flavoured liqueur (optional)

cocoa powder, for dusting

One Heat the cream in a pan without boiling; remove from the heat and stir in the chocolate. Leave for 2–3 minutes, then stir until melted and smooth. Stir in the spirit or liqueur, if using, and pour into a bowl. Chill until firm (about 2 hours).

Two Dust your hands with cocoa and shape teaspoonsful of the mixture into small balls. Roll in more cocoa, then wrap in foil to protect.

✱ VARY THE FLAVOUR:
For amaretti truffles, finely crush 50 g/2 oz amaretti biscuits. Stir into the cream and chocolate with 2 tablespoons Amaretto liqueur. Roll in crushed amaretti biscuits instead of cocoa.

✱ HOW TO WRAP IN STYLE:
For a simple pyramid box, to hold five foil-wrapped truffles overwrapped in tissue paper, take a 25 cm/10 in square of metallic card (from art shops). Score a central square measuring 7 cm/2¾ in for the base. Mark out 4 triangles from each side of the base. Cut around the triangles, then put the truffles on the base. Fold up the sides into a pyramid, punch a hole in the top of each triangle and tie with sparkly string; add a matching triangular-shaped tag.

Preparation: 20 minutes

ANTONIO CARLUCCIO'S

Neapolitan
Festive Ring *(Struffoli di Napoli)*

Antonio has fond memories of childhood Christmases when the family gathered round the table to make these sweet delicacies, nicknamed 'poor man's hazelnuts'. The finished ring is sure to impress friends and family. As Antonio says, 'If Neapolitans can't celebrate Easter without the *pastiera* – the Easter cake – it's even more unthinkable to celebrate Christmas without *struffoli*.'

Antonio is a much-loved TV cook, and the author of many top-selling books. *Antonio Carluccio's Italian Feast* won him a *Good Food* award for Favourite Cookery Book in 1997.

FOR THE DOUGH

5 medium eggs

3 tablespoons sugar

450 g/1 lb type 00 flour

grated rind of 1 lemon

grated rind of 1 orange

pinch of salt

1 tablespoon pure alcohol (if not available, use a strong vodka)

oil, for deep frying

FOR THE CARAMEL

½ orange and ½ lemon

250 g/9 oz orange blossom honey (about ½ jar)

100 g/4 oz sugar

FOR THE DECORATION

edible silver balls, silver leaf, angelica or candied peel (optional)

Preparation: 30 minutes, plus 2 hours resting
Cooking: 8–10 minutes
Serves: 10

One Make the dough for the *struffoli*: beat the eggs and sugar in a bowl. Mix in flour, citrus rind, salt and alcohol. Knead for 3–4 minutes (picture 1). Shape into a ball; cover and rest it for 2 hours in a cool place.

Two Take a little bit of the dough at a time and, using your hands, roll into sausage shapes about 1 cm/$\frac{1}{2}$ in in diameter (picture 2). Cut each sausage into pieces about the size of a hazelnut (picture 3). This is laborious so get friends and family to help. Toss the pieces of dough in a fine sprinkling of flour to stop them sticking (picture 4).

Three Pour some oil into a pan to a depth of about 2.5 cm/1in. Heat the oil and fry the *struffoli* for about 2–3 minutes until lightly brown and puffed up (picture 5) (do in batches). Remove with a slotted spoon. Drain on kitchen paper. Continue until all dough has been used.

Four Make the caramel: pare the rind from the orange and lemon (avoid any white pith) and cut into fine shreds. Put the honey and sugar in a heavy-based pan with 2 tablespoons of water. Heat gently until the liquid becomes clear. Add the shredded rinds, bring to the boil and simmer for a few minutes to make a light syrup. Add the *struffoli* (picture 6). Stir carefully until they are coated in syrup.

Five Arrange the *struffoli* in a ring on the plate.

Six Sprinkle with silver balls, silver leaf and angelica or candied peel, if using; leave to cool. The *struffoli* will keep in the syrup for up to a week in a polythene container with a lid. Store in a cool place.

✱ TYPE 00 OR DOPPIO ZERO FLOUR: This is superfine flour, sold in Italian delis and larger supermarkets, which gives the dough a light texture.

✱ USING THE RIGHT HONEY: Orange or lemon blossom, or acacia, gives the best flavour.

Canapés
without Tears

There's nothing more fiddly and time-consuming than making traditional canapés. Baking the classic array of mini-pastries, biscuits, baby quiches and puffs can take a whole day, and though they look beautiful and certainly show the skill (and patience) of the cook, there's an easier way that tastes just as good. Hence this fuss-free canapé guide, with just four basics – toasts, pastries, baby roast potatoes and chips – each transformed into something special, with mainly storecupboard ingredients.

Serve cold canapés first, then move on to hot. Finish with the chunky chips – they're irresistible. If you make the whole selection, you'll have enough for a drinks party for ten guests – though the recipes can easily be multiplied for larger gatherings. Some can be made ahead, some at the last minute – whatever suits you.

Timeplan for a 6.30pm drinks party

THE DAY BEFORE:

Make the toasts for the crostini; cool and store in an airtight container. Make the salsa; cover and chill.

ON THE DAY:

4.30pm

Make the Quick Guacamole and Herby Fromage Frais dips; cover and chill. Make the Mini Roast Potatoes; cool.

5.30pm

Prepare and cook the oven chips. Prepare the Savoury Puff Squares, but don't bake them; cover and chill. Remove chilled items from the fridge. Top all the crostini except the Prawn and Tomato Salsa.

JUST BEFORE SERVING:

Halve and put toppings on the potatoes (warm them first if you like). Top the Prawn and Tomato Crostini. Grill the Blue Cheese Mini Potatoes. Cook the Savoury Puffs at intervals during the evening.

Children are the best waiters on these occasions – but failing that, recruit a couple of friends as it's vital to keep nibbles moving.

Savoury Puff Squares

These are little pastry squares with four different toppings – if you're making bigger batches, cook each topping in succession while the last lot is being scoffed.

Preheat the oven to 200°C/ Gas 6/fan oven 180°C. Cut a 500 g packet of puff pastry in half and roll one half out to a 15 cm/ 6 in square. (Wrap the other half in plastic film and freeze for use in another recipe.) Trim slightly to straighten the edges, then cut into 16 small squares. Transfer to a lightly greased baking sheet. Add the toppings (see right) and bake for 10–15 minutes until the pastry is puffed and golden.

Preparation: 30–40 minutes
Cooking: 10–15 minutes
Makes: 16 puffs

THE TOPPINGS

✱ PEPPER AND PARMESAN
Divide 2 tablespoons of mixed pepper antipasti (from a jar) between 4 pastry squares. Sprinkle with a little black pepper and grated Parmesan.

✱ MUSHROOM AND MOZZARELLA
Divide 2 tablespoons of mixed mushroom antipasti (from a jar) between 4 pastry squares. Sprinkle 1 tablespoon of chopped fresh parsley and 25 g/1 oz mozzarella between the squares and season with a little black pepper.

✱ SPICY SAUSAGE AND SPINACH
Thaw 25 g/1 oz frozen leaf spinach, then squeeze out the excess moisture. Divide the spinach, 25 g/1 oz sliced chorizo sausage and 1 tablespoon of pine nuts between 4 pastry squares. Just before baking, drizzle over a little olive oil.

✱ TOMATO AND GOAT'S CHEESE
Roughly chop 1 small tomato, then divide between 4 pastry squares. Sprinkle with 25 g/1 oz crumbled goat's cheese.

Mini
Roast Potatoes

Small or baby potatoes are ideal for roasting and topping; served warm as canapés, they're truly tasty. You can cook the potatoes up to 2 hours ahead, but don't cut them in half. Let them cool completely, then cover and store in the fridge. Warm through before serving or serve at room temperature.

Preheat the oven to 190°C/Gas 5; fan oven: cook from cold at 170°C. Toss 8 small potatoes in 2 tablespoons of olive oil and tip into a roasting tin. Sprinkle with coarse sea salt and freshly ground black pepper, then roast for 30–40 minutes until tender. Leave the potatoes to stand until they are cool enough to handle, then split them in half lengthways.

Preparation: 30 minutes
Cooking: 30–40 minutes
Makes: 16 mini potatoes

THE TOPPINGS

✱ INSTANT CORONATION CHICKEN
Combine 25 g/1 oz roughly chopped cooked chicken and 1 tablespoon of chopped red pepper. Stir in 2 tablespoons of fromage frais, 1 teaspoon of curry paste, 2 teaspoons of mango chutney and 1 tablespoon of chopped parsley. Spoon on to 4 potatoes. Chill until needed.

✱ BLUE CHEESE AND CHIVES
Crumble 25 g/1 oz blue cheese and divide between 4 potato halves. Sprinkle over 1 tablespoon of chopped chives. Before serving, grill for 1–2 minutes until bubbling.

✱ SMOKED SALMON AND HORSERADISH
Mix 1 teaspoon of horseradish sauce with 1 tablespoon of crème fraîche and divide between 4 potato halves. Tear 25 g/1 oz smoked salmon into 8 pieces and put 2 on top of each potato half. Cover and chill until needed.

✱ CRÈME FRAÎCHE AND SPRING ONION
Season 2 tablespoons of crème fraîche with salt and pepper, then divide between 4 potato halves. Chop 2 spring onions, sprinkle over the potatoes, cover and chill. Just before serving, sprinkle with freshly ground black pepper.

Quick
Crostini

One small French stick is all you need to make the base of these easy nibbles. Look out for the thin French sticks rather than the traditional size, as they slice into the perfect-sized rounds for canapés. If you like, make the toasts the day before and cool completely; pack in an airtight container.

Preheat the oven to 190°C/Gas 5/fan oven 170°C. Cut a thin French stick into 16 slices about 5 mm/¼ in thick. Lay on a baking sheet and drizzle over 1–2 tablespoons of olive oil. Bake for 10 minutes until light golden.

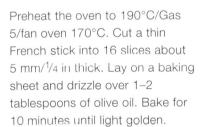

Preparation: 5 minutes
Cooking: 10 minutes
Makes: 16 crostini

THE TOPPINGS

✱ PRAWN AND TOMATO SALSA
Spoon a teaspoon each of the Easy Tomato Salsa (see page 65) on 4 of the toasts (no more than 10 minutes before serving or the toast will go soggy). Put a cooked tiger prawn on top of each; garnish each with a coriander leaf.

✱ PROSCIUTTO AND PEAR
Cut half a small pear into tiny dice and toss with 1 tablespoon of crème fraîche. Divide between 4 toasts. Tear 1 slice of prosciutto into 4 pieces and put on top of the pear mixture.

✱ FESTIVE TURKEY AND CRANBERRY
Divide 2 tablespoons of cranberry sauce between 4 toasts and spread not quite to the edges. Divide 25 g/1 oz chopped cooked turkey between the toasts and top each with a dollop of cranberry sauce. Sprinkle over snipped chives to garnish.

Chunky Oven Chips
and Dips

Chunky chips are the in thing – they are unfailingly popular as guests enjoy a second or third drink, especially when served with a selection of tasty dips.

MAKE THE CHIPS

Preheat the oven to 200°C/Gas 6; fan oven: cook from cold at 180°C. Scrub 4 175 g/6 oz potatoes and cut each into 8 wedges. Transfer to a roasting tin and drizzle over 3 tablespoons of olive oil. Season well, then sprinkle a good pinch of hot chilli powder over half of the potatoes and bake for 40–50 minutes, turning occasionally.

Preparation: 15 minutes
Cooking: 40–50 minutes
Serves: 10

VARY THE FLAVOURS

✳ ROSEMARY CHIPS: Sprinkle 1 tablespoon of chopped fresh rosemary over the potatoes before roasting.

✳ GARLIC CHIPS: Sprinkle over 3 finely chopped garlic cloves before roasting.

✳ LEMONY CHIPS: Tuck in lemon wedges between the potatoes before roasting.

The Dips

EASY TOMATO SALSA

A simple, not too spicy salsa that's not only served as a dip but is also used as a topping for the Prawn and Tomato Crostini and as a base for the Guacamole. If you like a spicier salsa, simply add another chilli. It can be made the day before you need it, kept covered and chilled.

Tip a 400 g can of chopped tomatoes in rich tomato juice into a food processor. Throw in a roughly chopped red chilli, 2 roughly chopped tomatoes, a small bunch of coriander, 2 garlic cloves, the rind and juice of 1 lime and 1 teaspoon of caster sugar. Whizz for about 20 seconds; taste and season. Cover and chill until needed.

Preparation: 10 minutes
Serves: 10

HERBY FROMAGE FRAIS

This refreshing dip uses a mixture of fresh parsley, dill, coriander and chives, but you can use whatever herbs you have to hand.

Mix 4 tablespoons of roughly chopped fresh herbs with 2 200 g tubs of fromage frais. Season lightly, cover and chill until needed (it can be made up to 2 hours ahead).

Preparation: 5 minutes
Serves: 10

QUICK GUACAMOLE

If you've made the salsa, you'll already have done most of the work for this dip – it's simply a case of whizzing it in the food processor with an avocado.

Halve, stone and peel a large ripe avocado, roughly chop the flesh and tip into a food processor. Spoon in 5 tablespoons of the Easy Tomato Salsa and whizz to a chunky purée. Transfer the guacamole to a small serving bowl and squeeze over the juice of 1 lime to prevent discoloration. Cover and chill until needed (it can be made up to 2 hours ahead).

Preparation: 5 minutes
Serves: 10

Jewelled
Madeira Cakes

FOR THE CAKE

350 g/12 oz butter, softened

350 g/12 oz caster sugar

6 medium eggs

425 g/15 oz self-raising flour

1 tablespoon baking powder

1 tablespoon vanilla essence

**finely grated rind of 2 oranges,
   plus 2 tablespoons juice**

FOR THE DECORATION

200 g/8 oz apricot jam

**1 kg/2 lb 4 oz yellow
   marzipan**

**300 g/10 oz icing sugar,
   plus extra**

**6 tablespoons Cointreau or
   other orange-flavoured
   liqueur**

250 g/9 oz luxury glacé fruits

**waxed or greaseproof paper
   and thin string**

Preparation: 1 hour
Cooking: 1 hour
Makes: 4 cakes about 13 cm/5 in
square

These exquisite mini-cakes – buttery Madeira wrapped in almond paste and steeped in a liqueur glaze – make beautiful gifts. They only keep for up to a week, so think ahead when you want to give them.

One Preheat the oven to 160°C/Gas 3/fan oven 150°C. Grease and line a 23 cm/9 in square cake tin. Beat together all the cake ingredients in a large bowl until creamy. Spoon into the tin, level the top and bake for about 1 hour until just firm and a skewer pushed into the centre comes out clean. Leave to cool in the tin.

Two Prepare the decoration: melt the jam in a pan over a medium heat, then press through a sieve. Peel the paper away from the cake and cut into four squares. (If the cake is domed, slice off the top to level.) Brush the sides with the glaze.

Three For each cake, thinly roll a quarter of the marzipan on a surface lightly dusted with icing sugar. Cut out 4 oblongs 1 cm/ 1/2 in taller than the cake itself. Press against the sides, making sure they stand above the cake top. Pinch together at the corners.

Four Beat together the icing sugar and liqueur to make a thin glaze. Spoon over half to flood the tops of the cakes. Decorate each with a few pieces of glacé fruit, then drizzle over the remaining glaze. Leave to set.

Five Wrap the cakes in 2 strips of waxed or greaseproof paper, to line the base and sides. Tie with string.

✱ HOW TO WRAP IN STYLE: Cut a 14 cm/5½ in square of thick card to support the base. Stand a cake on top and wrap with greaseproof paper or white tissue, then overwrap with cotton fabric. Secure with 2 lengths of satin ribbon, 60 cm/24 in long, knotted in the centre.

Festive
Almond Biscuits

These are light biscuits with a surprise almond filling and orange-scented sugar. They'll keep for up to a week in an airtight container, or freeze for up to 2 months.

Preparation: 30 minutes
Cooking: 20 minutes
Makes: 20

75 g/3 oz unsalted butter,

   chilled and cut into

   pieces, plus extra

115 g/4 oz self-raising flour

75 g/3 oz ground almonds

100 g/4 oz caster sugar

50 g/2 oz marzipan, cut into

   20 cubes

2 oranges

50 g/2 oz icing sugar

One Put the butter in a food processor with the flour and almonds. Whizz to fine breadcrumbs. Add half the caster sugar; whizz until the mixture starts to cling together, then work lightly into a ball with your hands.

Two Thinly roll out half of the dough between two pieces of plastic film on a lightly floured surface. Use a 6 cm/2½ in cutter to cut out crescents; put 10 on a greased baking sheet. Roll half the marzipan into sausages and lay on the crescents. Top each with another crescent (reroll trimmings if necessary) and seal the edges.

Three Make stars with remaining dough and marzipan. Chill for 30 minutes. Preheat the oven to 160°C/Gas 3/fan oven 150°C. Pare strips of orange rind, put on a baking sheet and bake for 3 minutes to dry slightly; cool. Mix the remaining caster sugar and the icing sugar; toss with the rind.

Four Bake biscuits for 18–20 minutes.; cool on a wire rack. Gently toss in a little of the orange sugar and pack; sprinkle with the remaining sugar.

✳ HOW TO WRAP IN STYLE: Decorate a terracotta pot with Magic Leaf. Use the bonding agent to paint on simple designs; leave for 15 minutes, then rub on the gold leaf. Push a square of metallic organza into the pot, fill with biscuits and tie with cord.

AINSLEY HARRIOTT'S

AINSLEY HARRIOTT'S
Roast Pork
with Chilli Mango Stuffing

Ainsley is a great friend of *Good Food* – he was the magazine's TV Personality of the Year in 1997 and 1998. He came up with this alternative roast for the Christmas table – a delicious stuffed pork dish – using lots of his favourite flavours such as chilli, lime and mango to make a wonderfully exuberant stuffing. The beauty of this dish is that it can be completely prepared the day before cooking and leftovers can be served cold with a big salad.

Preparation: 40 minutes, plus 2 hours marinating

Cooking: 45 minutes–1 hour

Serves: 6–8

FOR THE PORK AND MARINADE

1.8 kg/4 lb piece boned pork loin, scored

3 limes

2 garlic cloves

2 tablespoons soy sauce

3 tablespoons olive oil

5 cm/2 in piece root ginger

FOR THE STUFFING

225 g/8 oz day-old white bread, broken up

25 g/1 oz butter

4 tablespoons olive oil, plus extra for brushing

1 large red chilli, finely chopped

2.5 cm/1 in piece root ginger, grated

bunch of spring onions, sliced

1 glass white wine

large pinch ground allspice

100 g/4 oz dried mango slices

bay leaves, to garnish (optional)

FOR THE GRAVY

150 ml/¼ pint chicken or vegetable stock

sea salt and freshly ground black pepper

One Make the marinade: grate the rind from 2 of the limes and squeeze the juice from all 3. Finely chop the garlic and grate the ginger (picture 1).

Two Put the lime rind and juice, garlic and ginger in a bowl and stir in the soy sauce and olive oil.

Three Pour the marinade into a shallow non-metallic dish that is large enough to take the pork comfortably (picture 2). Add the pork, skin-side up (picture 3); cover with plastic film. Marinate in the fridge for at least 2 hours.

Four Preheat the oven to 230°C/Gas 8; fan oven: cook from cold at 210°C. Make the stuffing: whizz the bread to crumbs in a food processor.

Five Heat the butter and 2 tablespoons of oil in a frying pan (picture 4). Fry the chilli and ginger for 1 minute, stirring. Tip in the crumbs and fry over a fairly high heat for 4–5 minutes, tossing occasionally until golden (picture 5). Add the spring onions, wine and allspice and cook for 1 minute. Season, remove from the heat and leave to cool slightly.

Six Remove the pork from the marinade and dry the skin with kitchen paper; reserve the marinade. Cut a horizontal slice into the pork, open it out and lay the mango slices inside, then spoon on as much of the stuffing as you can. Bring up the sides of the meat to put it back together, and tie with string at 2.5 cm/1 in intervals (pictures 6 and 7).

Seven Wrap remaining stuffing in a foil parcel. Brush the pork skin lightly with olive oil and sprinkle evenly with sea salt.

Eight Heat the remaining oil in a roasting tin over a medium heat. Add the pork and sear all over until golden (picture 8) then roast for 20 minutes. Reduce to 190°C/Gas 5/ fan oven 170°C and cook for 45 minutes–1 hour.

Nine Transfer the pork to a chopping board and leave it to rest for 5–10 minutes. Put the roasting tin over a medium heat, pour in the reserved marinade and stock. Bring to the boil and simmer for 4–5 minutes until reduced by about a third. Slice the pork thickly (picture 9) and serve with gravy. Garnish with bay leaves, if liked.

✱ PREPARING AHEAD: Make the stuffing and leave to cool. When cold, stuff the pork and tie into a neat shape. Wrap in foil and store in the fridge for up to 2 days. Bring back to room temperature before roasting.

✱ COOKING WITH GINGER: If you use ginger in cooked dishes there's no need to peel it first as the skin will soften as it cooks.

✱ DRIED MANGO: This is sold in packets in the dried fruits and nuts section of the supermarket.

✱ PERFECT CRACKLING: Leg or loin joint is best for this. Get your butcher to score the skin for you about 1 cm/½ in apart (the finer the scoring, the crispier the crackling). Dry the skin, brush with a little oil and sprinkle with sea salt.

Mango and Almond
Trifle

FOR THE TRIFLE

350 g/12 oz Madeira or

sponge cake

3 tablespoons apricot jam or

conserve

140 g/5 oz whole blanched almonds

2 ripe mangoes

150 ml/¼ pint medium sherry

150 ml/¼ pint freshly squeezed

orange juice

25 g/1 oz caster sugar

FOR THE TOPPING

400 g carton fresh custard (or

use 425 ml/¾ pint home-made)

425 ml/¾ pint double cream

1 ripe mango

Preparation: 40 minutes, plus 2 hours chilling

Serves: 8

This is the perfect dessert for a special meal, and easy to make, too. The mangoes add a special touch – exotic fruits bring a memory of summer to a winter evening.

One Slice the cake thinly, then sandwich the slices together 2 at a time with the jam or conserve (picture 1). Toast the almonds in a dry frying pan until evenly browned. Peel, stone and chop the mangoes (pictures 2, 3). Arrange half the cake, half the almonds and half the mango chunks in a trifle bowl, then repeat the layers (picture 4).

Two Mix together the sherry, orange juice and sugar, then drizzle over the ingredients in the bowl (picture 5). Pour over the custard, cover and leave to soak in the fridge for at least 1 hour.

Three Whip the cream to stiff peaks and dollop large tablespoons over the custard (picture 6). Peel, stone and slice the remaining mango and slot the slices between each spoonful. Chill for 2 hours or until ready to serve.

✱ PREPARING AHEAD: The cake can be soaked and the custard poured over the day before serving; chill. With the cream and decoration in place, it can be chilled for up to 4 hours.

✱ WHEN IS A MANGO RIPE? This is tricky to judge. Start by sniffing it – if it emits a scent it may be ripe. Also, cradle it in your hand and squeeze gently; it should give slightly.

ANTONY WORRALL THOMPSON'S

Fabulous Ways
with Vegetables

If you're cooking a traditional turkey but want to serve some unusual veggie accompaniments, who better to work some magic than Antony Worrall Thompson? Everyone might expect Brussels sprouts – but Antony transforms these and other seasonal vegetables into something really special.

As well as making regular appearances on *Ready Steady Cook*, Antony is resident chef on *Food and Drink*. He also runs two highly-acclaimed restaurants with his wife, Jacinta.

Broccoli and
Leek Purée

85 g/3 oz unsalted butter

700 g/1 lb 9 oz leeks,
  washed and shredded

1 teaspoon soft fresh thyme
  leaves

225 g/8 oz potatoes, peeled
  and quartered

450 g/1 lb broccoli, stems
  sliced and florets separated

142 ml carton double cream

One Melt the butter in a large pan over a medium heat. Add the leeks and thyme. Cover, reduce the heat and cook for 15–20 minutes until the leeks are very soft.

Two Meanwhile, cook the potatoes in boiling salted water for 10–12 minutes until almost tender. Add the broccoli stems and cook for 5 minutes; add the florets and cook for 3 minutes more until tender.

Three Drain the potatoes and broccoli well and transfer to a food processor with the leeks. Process until smooth (you may have to do this in batches). Return the purée to a clean pan. Stir in the cream (picture 1), season and reheat gently just before serving.

✳ PREPARING AHEAD: Shred the leeks and trim the broccoli. Store in separate polythene bags in the fridge for up to a day. You could cook the dish beforehand, cool it and chill in the fridge for up to a day; then reheat it gently when required.

Preparation: 15 minutes
Cooking: 20 minutes
Serves: 6–8

Mushrooms and Chestnuts
in Cream

50 g/ 2 oz unsalted butter

700 g/1lb 9 oz chestnut

   mushrooms, quartered

6 tablespoons dry sherry

1 onion, finely chopped

1 teaspoon soft fresh thyme

   leaves

300 ml/½ pint chicken stock

142 ml carton double cream

450 g/1lb cooked whole

   chestnuts

One Melt half the butter in a heavy-based frying pan. Add the mushrooms (picture 1) and cook over a high heat, tossing occasionally, for 6–8 minutes until golden. Add the sherry and cook for a few minutes more until reduced. Remove from the pan; keep warm.

Two Heat the remaining butter in the same pan and add the onion and thyme. Cook over a medium heat for 3 minutes without browning. Pour in the chicken stock and simmer for 6 minutes.

Three Return the mushrooms to the pan (picture 2), stir in the cream and warm through. Fold in the chestnuts and season to taste. Warm through again to serve.

✱ PREPARING AHEAD: You can make the dish a few hours in advance, but don't add the chestnuts. Add them and warm through just before serving.

✱ BUYING CHESTNUTS: Cooked whole chestnuts are available from larger supermarkets, either vacuum packed or canned. For this recipe, you will need a 450 g vacuum pack or two 300 g cans.

Preparation: 10 minutes
Cooking: 20 minutes
Serves: 6–8

Corn
Pudding

25 g/1 oz unsalted butter

5 rashers streaky bacon,

   cut into thin strips

450 g/1 lb leeks,

   washed and shredded

1 red pepper, seeded

   and diced

3 corn cobs or

   300 g/10 oz frozen

2 tablespoons chopped

   fresh parsley

3 egg yolks

1 teaspoon prepared

   English mustard

600 ml/1 pint double cream

4 drops of Tabasco

splash of Worcestershire

   sauce

One Preheat the oven to 180°C/Gas 4; fan oven: cook from cold at 160°C. Melt the butter in a large pan over a medium heat. Add the bacon and cook for 2–3 minutes until crisp. Add the leeks and pepper and simmer for 3 minutes until any liquid has evaporated. Season to taste; stir in the corn and parsley. Put in a 1.2 litre/2 pint ovenproof dish.

Two In a bowl, whisk together the egg yolks, mustard and cream. Stir in the Tabasco and Worcestershire sauce. Pour over the corn mixture and bake for 45 minutes until golden and just set. Leave to cool for 10 minutes before serving.

✱ PREPARING AHEAD: This dish reheats well, and can be made a few hours in advance. Just before serving, reheat it in a 160°C/Gas 3/fan oven 140°C for 20–30 minutes.

✱ PREPARING CORN ON THE COB: Hold the corn upright on a board. Using a large sharp heavy knife, slice down through the cob to remove the niblets (picture 1). Turn the cob and repeat until all the niblets are removed. Cook for 5 minutes in boiling water, then drain and use. Do not add salt to the cooking water as this toughens the corn.

Preparation: 40 minutes
Cooking: 45 minutes
Serves: 6–8

Christmas
Brussels

450 g/1 lb Brussels sprouts,

   trimmed

85 g/3 oz unsalted butter

1 small onion, finely

   chopped

½ teaspoon fennel seeds

grated rind of 1 orange

½ teaspoon soft fresh

   thyme leaves

175 g/6 oz cooked

   chestnuts, halved

One Cook the sprouts in a pan of boiling salted water for 6 minutes.

Two Heat the butter in a frying pan. Add the onion, fennel seeds, orange rind and thyme and cook for a few minutes until the onions start to colour (picture 1).

Three Tip in the drained sprouts and chestnuts (picture 2) and fry until the sprouts are slightly tinged with brown. Season to taste and serve at once.

✱ PREPARING AHEAD: Trim sprouts and store in a polythene bag in the fridge for up to 2 days. If you want to cook the sprouts ahead, drain them after boiling and plunge them into iced water; then drain again and chill. (This stops cooking and sets the colour.)

✱ COOKING YOUR OWN CHESTNUTS: The easiest way is to put six on a plate, split each and cook on High in the microwave for 1 minute. Continue until all are cooked, then peel and use. Alternatively, split them and bake in a moderate oven for 15–20 minutes before peeling.

Preparation: 20 minutes
Cooking: 15 minutes
Serves: 6

Turkey and all
the Trimmings

To help the big day go smoothly for you –
we have included a shopping list of key
ingredients (page 96), while my timeplan
(opposite) will help you stay calm.

   Buttery lemon and lime add a zesty twist to
the traditional turkey, while accompaniments
also get wonderful flavour boosts.

On the menu

- BUTTER-BASTED LEMON AND LIME TURKEY

- CHESTNUT-STUFFED RED ONIONS

- ROSEMARY AND GARLIC ROASTIES

- SAUSAGEMEAT AND THYME KOFTAS

- HONEY MUSTARD PARSNIPS

- PORT AND ORANGE GRAVY

- CRANBERRY SAUCE (SEE PAGE 51)

- BREAD SAUCE

Timeplan for a 2pm lunch

THE DAY BEFORE

Make and chill lemon and lime butter for turkey
Make turkey stock; chill
Make the koftas, wrap in foil and chill
Stuff red onions, cover; keep in a cool place

ON THE DAY

8.30am

Preheat the oven
Butter the turkey breast and truss

9am

Put turkey in to roast
Prepare parsnips and potatoes for the oven

10am

Baste turkey with the pan juices every ½ hour
Infuse milk for bread sauce

12.30pm

Put potatoes in oven
Cook onions

1.00pm

Remove foil from turkey; cover breast with bacon

1.30pm

If turkey is cooked, put on a platter; cover with foil
Put kottas in oven
Make gravy

2pm

Serve lunch: enjoy!

Butter-basted
Lemon and Lime Turkey

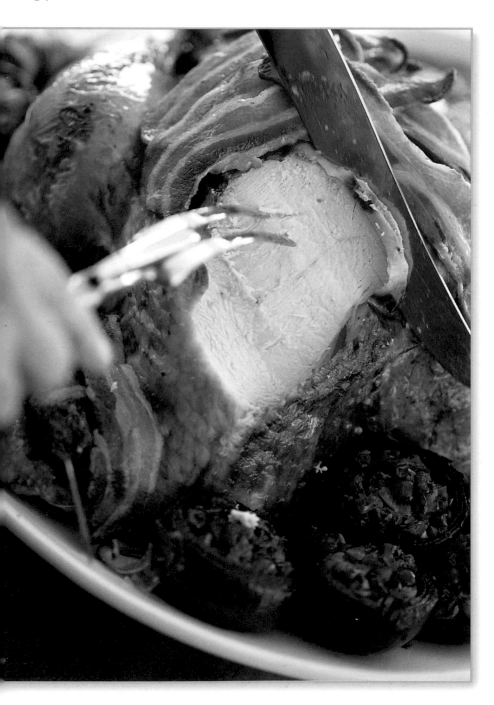

The problem of dry breast meat is neatly solved by sliding a layer of lemon and lime butter under the skin, while the comprehensive roasting chart given on page 93 will ensure the cooking time is just right.

1 lemon

1 lime

85 g/3 oz softened butter

5.6 kg/12 lb oven-ready turkey, thawed if frozen

1 onion

225 g/8 oz streaky bacon

bay leaves and thyme sprigs, to garnish

Preparation: 30 minutes

Cooking: time varies according to size of bird

Serves: 10–12

One Grate the rind from the citrus fruits, reserving the flesh. In a bowl, mix together the butter, lemon and lime rinds and season. Spread the butter over a sheet of foil big enough to cover the area of the turkey breast (picture 1). Cover with another sheet of foil and press down to make an even layer of butter. Chill until firm.

Two Preheat the oven to 180°C/Gas 4; fan oven: cook from cold at 160°C. Remove the giblets from the turkey (reserve for the stock and gravy) and wash the bird inside and out. Dry well with kitchen paper. Quarter the lemon and lime, peel and halve the onion. Put these in the cavity of the bird.

Three Loosen the skin of the breast by sliding your hands (take off rings first) between the flesh and the skin – not a pleasant job, but worth doing. Peel the foil from the chilled butter (keep one piece of foil for step 4) then slide it between the breast and skin (picture 2) (it will break up a bit but this is easier than spreading soft butter). Smooth the skin back over the butter then season the turkey generously inside and out. Tie the legs together at the top of the drumsticks to give the turkey a neat shape.

Four Weigh the bird to calculate the cooking time – allow 20 minutes per 450 g/1 lb, plus 20 minutes extra (see page 93). Put the turkey in a dry roasting tin and loosely cover the breast with a sheet of the buttered foil (picture 3). Do not enclose the whole turkey in foil.

Five Roast the turkey for the calculated cooking time, basting with the pan juices every 30–40 minutes. Half an hour before the end of cooking, remove the foil to crisp the skin, baste with the pan juices and lay the bacon in a lattice over the breast (picture 4).

Six To test if the turkey is cooked, pierce the thigh with a skewer at the thickest part. If the juices run clear it is done; if they are a little pink, give it 15 minutes more, then test again. Transfer to a serving platter and cover tightly with foil; rest for 15 minutes to make carving easier.

Seven Spoon off as much fat as possible from the tin, then measure out 175 ml/6 fl oz of the remaining pan juices to make the gravy (page 90); arrange the Chestnut-stuffed Red Onions, and Sausagemeat and Thyme Koftas around the bird and garnish with bay and thyme.

✱ MAKING TURKEY STOCK: Rinse the giblets and put them in a pan with a quartered onion, chopped celery stick, chopped carrot, a few black peppercorns, teaspoon of salt, bay leaf and parsley sprig. Cover with 850 ml/ 1½ pints water and bring to the boil. Skim off any scum, then reduce the heat and partly cover. Simmer for 1 hour then strain.

✱ PREPARING AHEAD: Make this stock up to 2 days ahead. Cool it quickly, then cover and put in the fridge until ready to use. Any left over can be frozen for up to 3 months.

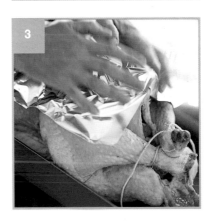

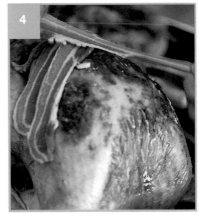

Chestnut-stuffed
Red Onions

6 medium red onions

3 tablespoons olive oil,
plus extra

1 tablespoon balsamic
vinegar

1 celery stick, finely
chopped

1 garlic clove, finely
chopped

85 g/3 oz fresh or frozen
cranberries

200 g/8 oz cooked peeled
chestnuts, finely chopped

25 g/1 oz chopped fresh
parsley or coriander

Preparation: 30 minutes
Cooking: 1 hour 5 minutes
Makes: 12

One Preheat the oven to
180°C/Gas 4/fan oven 160°C. Peel
the onions (keep the root intact),
and cut each one in half through
the middle. Remove several layers
from the centre of each half using a
teaspoon and a sharp knife
(picture 1). Cover any holes in the
bottom with a small slice of onion.
Finely chop half the removed onion
layers (use the rest another time).

Two Arrange the onion halves,
cut-side up, in one layer in an oiled
ovenproof dish. Whisk together
2 tablespoons of the oil with the
balsamic vinegar, salt and pepper.
Brush or drizzle evenly over the
onions (picture 2), then cover with
foil and bake for 45 minutes until
the onions are almost tender.

Three Fry the reserved finely
chopped onion in the remaining oil
with the celery for about 5 minutes
until softened. Add the garlic and
cranberries and cook gently for
6–8 minutes until the cranberries
start to soften; remove from the
heat and stir in the chestnuts,
parsley or coriander, salt and
pepper.

Four Spoon the chestnut mixture
into the onion shells (picture 3) and
return to the oven for 20 minutes
(picture 4).

Rosemary and
Garlic Roasties

1.6 kg/3½ lb floury potatoes,

   e.g. Maris Piper

4 tablespoons olive oil

2 garlic cloves, chopped

4 tablespoons fresh

   rosemary, chopped

One Peel the potatoes and cut them into chunks. Pat dry with kitchen paper (picture 1). In a bowl, mix together the oil, garlic and half the rosemary, and season.

Two Spread the potatoes out in a roasting tin and drizzle over the rosemary and garlic oil. Stir around to thoroughly coat the potatoes (picture 2); sprinkle the rest of the rosemary over the top. Cook on the shelf above the turkey for 1–1½ hours until crisp and golden.

Preparation: 10 minutes

Cooking: 1–1½ hours

Serves: 12

Sausagemeat and
Thyme Koftas

2 tablespoons olive oil

1 small onion, finely

    chopped

450 g/1 lb good quality

    sausagemeat

grated rind of 1 lemon

100 g/4 oz fresh white

    breadcrumbs

2 teaspoons chopped fresh

    thyme or 1 teaspoon dried,

    plus extra sprigs

1 egg, beaten

12 rashers rindless thin-cut

    streaky bacon

12 wooden or metal skewers

One Heat the olive oil in a small pan, then add the onion and fry gently for about 5 minutes, until softened and lightly browned. Remove from the heat and cool. In a bowl, mix together the meat, lemon rind, breadcrumbs and thyme (picture 1). Add the onion and oil, then add the egg and mix well, squeezing the mixture between your hands until everything is evenly mixed.

Two Divide into 12 equal pieces – they should weigh about 140 g/ 5 oz each. Press each portion around a skewer to make a sausage shape. Wrap a bacon rasher loosely around each kofta, tucking a thyme sprig between the folds (picture 2).

Three Put in a roasting tin or other shallow oven-proof dish (picture 3), and roast for 35 minutes, turning after 20 minutes.

✱ PREPARING AHEAD: These koftas can be made the day before and kept in the fridge wrapped in foil. Alternatively, wrap closely in freezer foil and freeze for up to a month.

Preparation:	45 minutes
Cooking:	35 minutes
Makes:	12

Honey Mustard
Parsnips

6–8 parsnips, peeled and quartered lengthways

2 tablespoons olive oil

2 tablespoons mustard seeds, brown or white

2 tablespoons clear honey

One Cut any woody parts from the centre of the parsnips and discard. In a bowl whisk together the oil, mustard seeds, honey, salt and pepper (picture 1).

Two Put the parsnips in a roasting tin, drizzle over the flavoured oil and toss together until they are evenly coated (picture 2). Cook for 40–50 minutes until golden.

✱ PREPARING AHEAD: Prepare the parsnips and store in a polythene bag in the fridge for up to a day.

Preparation: 10 minutes
Cooking: 40–50 minutes
Serves: 12

Port and Orange
Gravy

175 ml/6 fl oz turkey pan
juices

2 tablespoons plain flour

850 ml/1½ pints turkey stock
(see page 85)

300 ml/½ pint port

grated rind and juice of 1
orange

1 tablespoon prepared
mustard

One Heat the pan juices in the
roasting tin, stir in the flour and
cook for 2 minutes. Stir in the
stock and port and simmer for
5 minutes (picture 1).

Two Stir in the orange rind and
juice and plenty of seasoning.
Bring to the boil, stirring, then stir
in the mustard (picture 2). Simmer
for a further 5 minutes, uncovered,
until slightly thickened and glossy.

Preparation: 5 minutes
Cooking: 15 minutes
Serves: 10–12

Bread
Sauce

600 ml/1 pint full fat milk

50 g/2 oz butter

1 onion, finely chopped

6 whole cloves

2 garlic cloves

1 bay leaf

3 fresh thyme sprigs

100 g/4 oz fresh white
  breadcrumbs

4–5 tablespoons single
  cream (optional but lovely)

In a pan, simmer the milk, butter, onion, cloves, garlic and herbs for 20 minutes (picture 1). Strain (picture 2); return the milk to the pan. Add the breadcrumbs (picture 3) and simmer for 3–4 minutes. Season well with salt and pepper, then stir in the cream (picture 4), if using. Serve warm.

✱ PREPARING AHEAD: The components for this sauce can all be prepared ahead ready for the final assembly. Make and freeze the breadcrumbs up to 3 months ahead. Earlier in the day infuse the milk and strain it.

Preparation: 5 minutes
Cooking: 35 minutes
Serves: 12

All You ever Wanted to Know
about Turkey

The arrival of that bird prompts a hundred questions – all of which are answered here.

WHAT SIZE TURKEY?

Allow 350–450 g/12 oz–1 lb per serving for birds up to 4.5 kg/10 lb; 200–350 g/8–12 oz for birds over 4.5 kg/10 lb (allows for leftovers).

HOW LONG WILL IT KEEP?

Supermarket fresh turkeys have a use-by date. If you buy yours from the butcher, ask how long it will keep – in general, cook within 3 days. Store loosely wrapped in a dish that will catch any drips, at the bottom of the fridge, or covered in a cold place.

FROZEN OR FRESH?

Frozen turkeys can be stored in the freezer for up to 6 months. They are much cheaper than fresh, and some are even self-basting – the turkeys are injected with sunflower oil or butter, which seeps into the meat during cooking for optimum succulence. However, they do need to be thawed carefully (see chart on page 93). A fresh bird will inevitably have a finer flavour than a frozen one.

HOW TO BUY THE BEST TURKEY

Whether buying fresh or frozen, look for a bird with a good plump breast as a scrawny bird will not be as tender. In any case, most people prefer breast meat to leg – even though the latter has a richer flavour.

When buying frozen, check that the packaging is intact and ensure that the bird is completely frozen and hasn't started to thaw.

Remember a turkey is only as good as its feed. It's worth paying extra for a corn-fed bird as its meat will have superior flavour and texture.

Don't be taken in by appearances. A smooth, white skin is not always an indication of quality. In fact, free-range birds have tougher feathers which often leave stubs in the skin. These may not look very pretty, but don't bother trying to remove them. They don't do any harm, and their presence suggests a succulent bird with flavoursome skin.

If ordering your turkey from a local butcher, ask him whether he or his suppliers hang their turkeys. Proper hanging improves the flavour and tenderness of the meat.

If you want a free-range or gourmet turkey, don't be fooled by fancy labels that may not mean anything at all. Labels such as 'farm reared' or 'farm fresh' don't have any legal definition. Instead, look out for turkeys carrying a Golden Promise label at your local butcher -these are produced by members of the Traditional Farmfresh Turkey Association, which has stringent rules governing the quality of the birds its members raise. Free-range or otherwise, the turkeys are slow-growing breeds, which develop most flavour and are properly hung.

DEFROSTING A FROZEN BIRD

Thaw your turkey on a tray, in its packaging, in a cool place such as a larder or garage. When completely thawed (check for ice crystals in the cavity) remove the packaging, giblets and neck, wipe with kitchen paper and store, loosely covered with plastic film or greaseproof paper, in the fridge at a temperature of no more than 5°C.

HOW LONG TO COOK IT FOR

As a guide, allow 20 minutes per 450 g/1 lb, plus an extra 20 minutes cooking. Above 6.75 kg/15 lb, allow 15 minutes per 450 g/1 lb, plus 15 minutes. If stuffing the turkey, reweigh after stuffing to calculate times. If your scales can't cope, bring the bathroom scales into the kitchen, get someone to stand on them, hand them the turkey and note the difference. Cover the turkey loosely with foil and cook at 180°C/Gas 4; fan oven: cook from cold at 160°C.

COOKING AND THAWING TIMES

WEIGHT OF THE BIRD	THAWING	COOKING TIME
1.3–2.25 kg/3–5 lb	20 hours	1 hour 20 minutes–2 hours
2.7–3.3 kg/6–7 lb	22 hours	2 hours 20 minutes–2 hours 40 minutes
3.6–4 kg/8–9 lb	24+ hours	3 hours–3 hours 20 minutes
4.5–5 kg/10–11 lb	24+ hours	3 hours 40 minutes–4 hours
5.5–6 kg/12–13 lb	25+ hours	5–6 hours
6.4–7 kg/14–17 lb	30+ hours	5–6 hours
8.2–9 kg/18–20 lb	45+ hours	6 hours 20 mins–7 hours

Nowadays turkeys tend to be cooked for shorter times than was once recommended. Many top chefs opt for shorter times still; but I can't recommend doing this at home as the turkey may not be fully cooked. The times given above should make sure your bird is cooked through without it being overdone or dry.

STUFFING TURKEY

Stuff the neck end only, never the body cavity, as the temperature in the centre of the bird may not rise high enough to destroy any food poisoning bacteria. The safest way to cook stuffing is in a separate dish.

THE SECRET OF A REALLY TASTY TURKEY

If you're not cooking the recipe on page 84, where the bird is basted with butter, then it's a good idea to roast your turkey upside-down on its breast; this enables the juices from the back and legs to run down to the breast, keeping it moist. To prevent the flesh drying out, baste the bird with butter or olive oil, cover loosely with a sheet of foil and baste every 30–40 minutes. Remove the foil for the last 40 minutes of cooking time to crisp the skin.

Cook a smaller bird in a large roasting bag. Remove from bag for the last 30 minutes and baste.

To check that your turkey is fully cooked, pierce the thickest part of the thigh with a skewer. Leave for a minute – initial juices may be clouded with fat, then the juices should run clear. If you have a meat thermometer, check that the centre of the bird has reached 75°C/167°F to ensure any salmonella is destroyed.

When the turkey is cooked, remove from the oven, cover with either foil or a clean cloth and leave to rest (see timeplan, page 83). This makes carving easier and the turkey will become more succulent; it also gives you time to make the gravy.

HOW TO MAKE WONDERFUL TURKEY GRAVY

Again, if you're not cooking my Port and Orange Gravy, this makes the more traditional version. First make giblet stock: rinse the giblets and put in a pan with 600 ml/1 pint cold water, half an onion, a carrot and a celery stick, a few black peppercorns, 2 bay leaves and a few parsley and/or thyme sprigs. Bring to the boil, then reduce the heat and simmer, partly covered, for 1 hour. Strain and cool. When cold, chill for up to 1 day before use, or freeze.

To make the gravy, put the bird on a carving plate and cover. Pour off the fat from the roasting tin, leaving just the meat juices and 1 tablespoon of fat, then set the tin on the hob over a medium heat and stir in 1 tablespoon of plain flour. Cook for 1 minute, stirring and scraping up any bits from the bottom of the tin with a wire whisk. Gradually stir in the stock, then add a splash of wine if you wish and season with salt and pepper. Pour any juices from the turkey into the gravy. Let it simmer while the turkey rests and is carved, by which time the gravy will be ready to serve.

SAVING THE LEFTOVERS

Cool leftover turkey quickly by putting it on a cold plate and letting it stand in a cool place. When cold, wrap well in foil or plastic film, then store in the fridge for up to 3 days. Meat removed from the bone may also be frozen, packed in freezer bags or boxes, for up to 2 months. Meat frozen in gravy will be moister.

Mince Pies

Gluten-free flour makes crumbly pastry, so for best results roll it out between sheets of non-stick baking parchment or plastic film. Store and freeze like normal mince pies.

280 g/10 oz gluten-free flour

140 g/5 oz butter, plus extra

2 tablespoons caster sugar

250 g/9 oz gluten-free mincemeat

a little milk, for glazing

3 tablespoons flaked almonds

Preparation: 25 minutes, plus 5 minutes cooling

Cooking: 15 minutes

Makes: 12

One Preheat the oven to 200°C/Gas 6/fan oven 180°C. Lightly grease a 12-hole bun tin with butter. Sift the flour into a bowl, then rub in the butter until the mixture resembles coarse breadcrumbs. Stir in half the sugar, then add about 2 tablespoons of water and mix to a soft but not sticky dough. (If it's too soft to handle, wrap and chill for 30 minutes.)

Two Roll out the pastry and cut out 12 pie bases using a 7 cm/2^{3}/$_{4}$ in plain or fluted cutter. Transfer these rounds to the bun tin and fill with heaped teaspoonfuls of mincemeat. Cut 12 slightly smaller rounds (about 6 cm/^{1}/$_{2}$ in) for lids. Moisten the edge of each base with water and affix the lids, pressing the edges to seal. Brush the tops with a little milk and scatter over a few almonds. Sprinkle with the remaining sugar and bake for 15 minutes. Cool the mince pies in the tin for 5 minutes before removing, as they crumble if removed while still warm.

Christmas Pudding

140 g/5 oz fresh gluten-free
   bread

100 g/4 oz butter, melted,
   plus extra

50 g/2 oz rice flour

½ teaspoon ground cinnamon

1 teaspoon mixed spice

½ teaspoon gluten-free
   baking powder

100 g/4 oz cooking apple,
   peeled and grated

400 g/4 oz carrot, grated

400 g/14 oz mixed dried fruit

100 g/4 oz light muscovado
   sugar

50 g/2 oz chopped mixed peel

50 g/2 oz ground almonds

1 tablespoon black treacle

2 eggs, beaten

finely grated rind of ½ lemon
   and ½ orange

2 tablespoons sherry
   (optional)

One Break the bread into pieces and whizz to fine crumbs in a food processor; set aside. Grease and line the base of a 1.2–1.4 litre/ 2–2½ pint pudding basin with greaseproof paper. Sift together the rice flour, spices and baking powder. Add the melted butter, apple, carrot, dried fruit, breadcrumbs, sugar, peel and almonds. Mix thoroughly.

Two Heat the treacle until just warm. Remove from the heat and stir in the eggs, citrus rind and sherry, if using. Mix into the flour and fruit, then spoon the mixture into the prepared basin. Cover with a double thickness of greaseproof paper, tie to secure and overlap foil. Put into a large pan and pour in boiling water to come one-third of the way up the basin. Bring to the boil, then cover and steam for 4 hours, until the pud is risen and firm to the touch. Cool completely, then top with greaseproof paper, wrap in foil and keep in a cool dry place. To reheat, steam for 2 hours.

Preparation: 25 minutes

Cooking: 4 hours, plus 2 hours reheating on day of serving

Serves: 8

Shopping list

MEAT

5.6 kg/12 lb oven-ready turkey
450 g/1 lb good quality sausages
   or sausagemeat
225 g/8 oz streaky bacon
12 rashers rindless thin-cut streaky bacon

GROCERIES

1 bottle port
small white loaf
1 egg
200 g vacuum pack of
   cooked peeled chestnuts
olive oil
balsamic vinegar
mustard
plain flour
peppercorns
mustard seeds
clear honey
sugar

FRUIT, VEGETABLES AND HERBS

1.6 kg/3½ lb floury potatoes
6–8 parsnips
3 onions
1 carrot and 2 celery sticks
6 medium red onions
2 bay leaves
thyme sprigs
rosemary
parsley
coriander (optional)
1 orange
2 lemons
1 lime
garlic
325 g/11 oz fresh or frozen cranberries
6 whole cloves

DAIRY

140 g/5 oz butter
142 ml carton single cream
600 ml/1 pint full fat milk

EXTRAS

12 wooden or metal skewers
foil

MARY CADOGAN is an experienced cookery writer with a wealth of experience in many areas of the food world. Before joining *BBC Good Food Magazine*, Mary contributed regularly to several national magazines and was a top food stylist specialising in food photography. She is also the author of several best-selling cookery books. Mary was appointed Deputy Editor of *Good Food* in 1993 and since then, in addition to writing her popular food features in the magazine, she has been responsible for ensuring that all the recipes taste great, work perfectly and are beautifully photographed.

Published by BBC Worldwide Ltd,
Woodlands, 80 Wood Lane,
London W12 OTT

First published in 1999

Additional photography
Chocolate Chestnut Log (page 26): Linda Burgess
Canapés without Tears (pages 60–5): Philip Webb
Christmas on a Special Diet (pages 94–5): William Reavell
Edible Gifts (pages 16, 17, 28, 54, 55, 66, 68): Simon Smith
Glazed Ham with Caramelized Fruits (page 42): Martin Thompson
(all photographs © BBC Worldwide, 1999)

All the recipes in this book have been previously published in
BBC Good Food Magazine

ISBN: 0 563 55109 7

Project Editor: Rachel Brown
Copy-editor: Christine King
Designers: John Calvert and Isobel Gillan
Cover designer: Jason Vrakas

Set in Helvetica
Printed and bound in Great Britain by
Butler & Tanner Limited, Frome and London
Colour separations by Radstock Reproductions Limited,
Midsomer Norton
Cover printed by Belmont Press, Northampton

Back cover photographs
TOP: *Canapés* (pages 60–5)
CENTRE: *Turkey and all the Trimmings* (pages 82–91)
BOTTOM: *Festive Mince Pies* (pages 20–1)